WORLD BOOK'S

YOUNG SCIENTIST

WORLD BOOK'S

YOUNG SCIENTIST

- **HUMAN BODY**
- **CONSERVATION**

2

World Book, Inc.
a Scott Fetzer company
Chicago

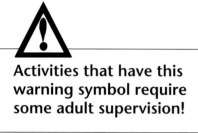

**Activities that have this
warning symbol require
some adult supervision!**

The quest to explore the known world and to describe its creation and
subsequent development is nearly as old as mankind. In the Western
world, the best-known creation story comes from the book of Genesis.
It tells how God created Earth and all living things. Modern religious
thinkers interpret the Biblical story of creation in various ways. Some
believe that creation occurred exactly as Genesis describes it. Others
think that God's method of creation is revealed through scientific
investigation. *Young Scientist* presents an exciting picture of what
scientists have learned about life and the universe.

World Book, Inc.
233 N. Michigan Avenue
Chicago, IL 60601

**For information on other World Book products,
call 1-800-WORLDBK (967-5325), or visit us at our
Web site at http://www.worldbook.com**

© 1997, 1995, 1991, 1990 World Book, Inc.

ISBN: 0-7166-2752-3 (volume II)
ISBN: 0-7166-2797-3 (set)

Library of Congress Catalog Card No. 00-107193

Printed in the United States of America

1 2 3 4 5 6 7 06 05 04 03 02 01 00

Contents

Human Body

Conservation

HUMAN BODY

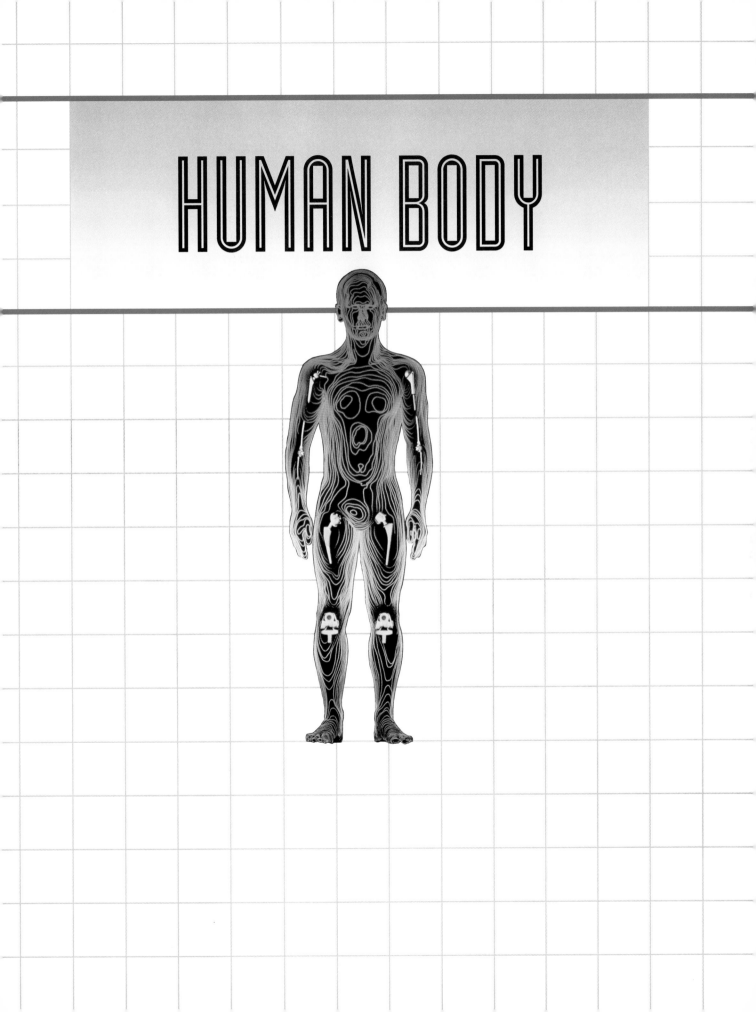

Your living body

People are of different shapes and sizes—and different colors, too. Some are tall, some are short, and others are somewhere in between. Some have curly hair, some straight hair. Skin can be dark or light brown, yellowish or pinkish white. Eyes can be brown, blue, green, or gray.

Sometimes people look like each other, especially if they are from the same family. They are even more alike if they are identical twins. But no two people are exactly the same. Everyone has his or her own special shape and unique fingerprints, footprints, and voice.

Inside your body

In many ways, your body is like a wonderful machine. Each of the many different parts of your body has a special job to do. Your bones and muscles work together to make you move. Your heart pumps blood around your body. Your lungs take in a gas called oxygen from the air. The most complicated part of your body is your brain, which controls all the other parts. Along with your nervous system, your brain keeps your body working.

Machines need fuel to make them work. For example, cars need gasoline. The fuel for the human machine is food. You need a regular supply of food to keep your body working properly.

Of course, you're not really a machine because you're alive. You have a living body. You grow like other living things do. But no other kind of animal can think, feel, and talk like you can. You are a unique living thing.

Your body is like a machine. All the parts work together
smoothly to make this gymnast turn and flip.

Find out more by looking
at pages **20–21**
40–41

What's your body made of?

Like all other living things, your body is made of tiny parts called **cells.** Most cells are so small that you can see them only with the help of a microscope. There are many trillions of cells in your body. Your skin, blood, muscles, and most other parts of you are made of cells.

Cells are made of a jellylike substance called **cytoplasm** and a nucleus. Cells are alive. They make new cells by dividing in two. Every day, your body makes about two billion new cells, but at the same time about two billion old cells die. This helps your body to keep itself in good working order.

This photograph shows three nerve cells in a human brain. The branches coming out from the cells carry messages to other parts of the body.

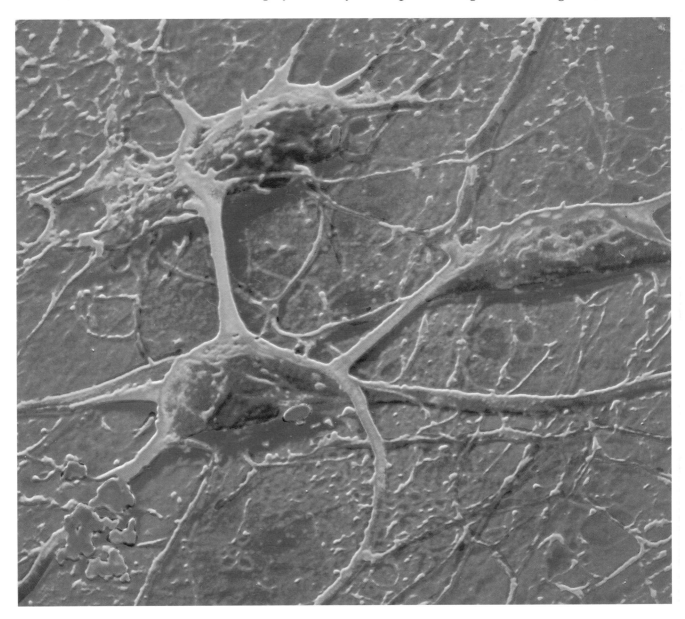

Different cells have different jobs

Cells have different shapes and sizes because they do different jobs. The cells in your muscles are long and stretchy. Many blood cells are round. Nerve cells are long and thin, with lots of branches like a tree. Nerve cells carry messages to and from your brain.

Cells of the same kind and function join together to make a material called **tissue.** Different kinds of tissue join together to make parts of your body called **organs.** You have many different organs, such as your eyes, your heart, and your brain.

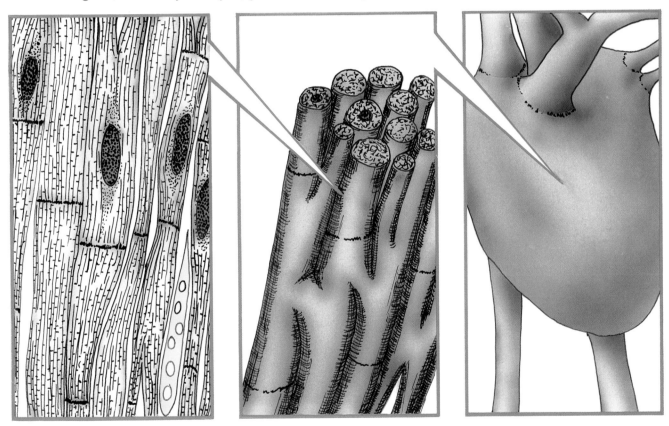

1. Long, stretchy muscle cells are grouped together.

2. Muscle cells join together to form muscle tissue. This consists of bunches of threadlike fibers.

3. Muscle tissues like this make up the walls of the heart. This organ pumps blood all around your body.

How much of your body is water?
About two-thirds of your body is made up of water. This lies in and around your tissues and organs.

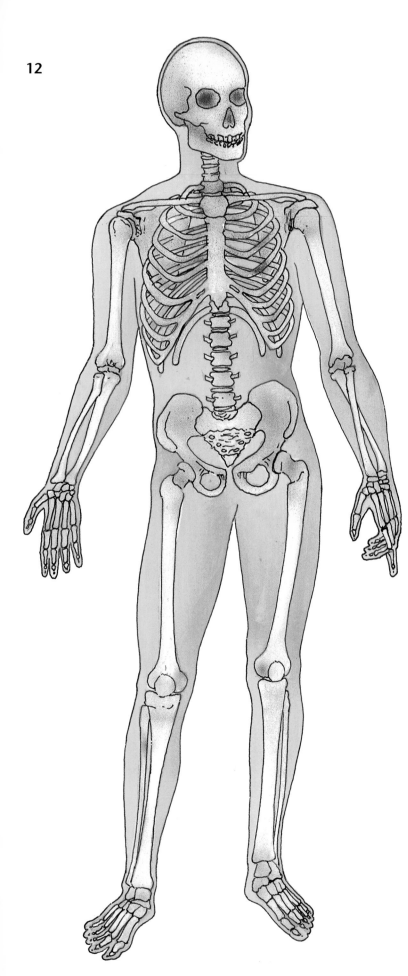

Your body's framework

You have about 200 bones in your body. They are joined together to make up the **skeleton.** Your skeleton helps give your body its shape. The bones of your skull determine the shape of your head. Long bones hold muscles that shape your arms and legs. Rib bones curve to make the sides of your chest. Your skeleton is the framework of your body. It holds you up and also helps you to move around.

Some bones protect your main inner organs. For example, your skull protects your brain. And your ribs make a cage around your heart and lungs.

What are bones made of?

Bones are hard tissues that are living parts of your body, just as your brain and heart are living parts. Bones contain cells that divide and multiply, causing you to grow. These cells are also always rebuilding the bony tissue to keep it strong. Rebuilding happens less as people grow older. So a broken bone will often heal much more quickly in a child than in an adult.

Bones store substances called **minerals,** which your body uses. Calcium is a mineral. It helps to make the bones hard.

Bones have a strong covering, called **periosteum.** Inside, there is a hard layer of **compact bone.** A long bone, such as the thigh bone, has spongy tissue at its ends, called **cancellous bone,** and soft **marrow** in its hollow center.

Some parts of your skeleton, such as your arms and legs, have only a few long bones. Other parts, such as your hands and feet, have many small bones.

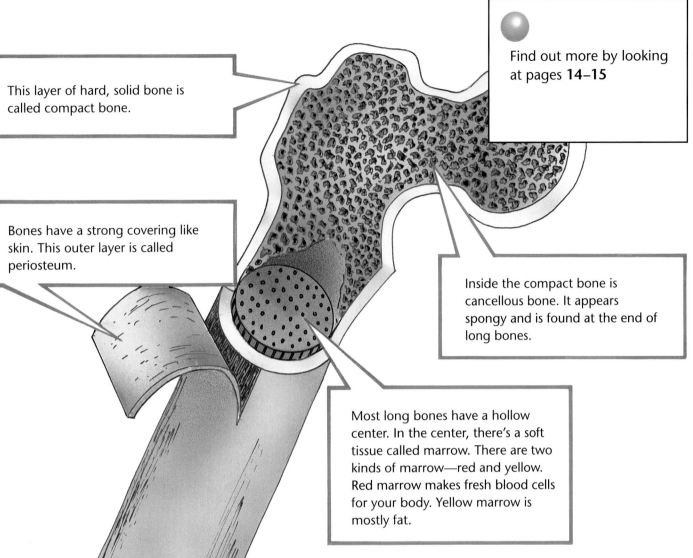

This layer of hard, solid bone is called compact bone.

Find out more by looking at pages **14–15**

Bones have a strong covering like skin. This outer layer is called periosteum.

Inside the compact bone is cancellous bone. It appears spongy and is found at the end of long bones.

Most long bones have a hollow center. In the center, there's a soft tissue called marrow. There are two kinds of marrow—red and yellow. Red marrow makes fresh blood cells for your body. Yellow marrow is mostly fat.

How are bones held together?

Your bones are held together by strong, flexible straps called **ligaments.** The ends of the bones are covered with a smooth, rubbery substance called **cartilage.** This is the same kind of substance that forms the tip of your nose. Cartilage works like a cushion so that the bones don't grind against each other. Cartilage is covered in a liquid called **synovial fluid.** This keeps the bones moving smoothly, like oil in the parts of a machine.

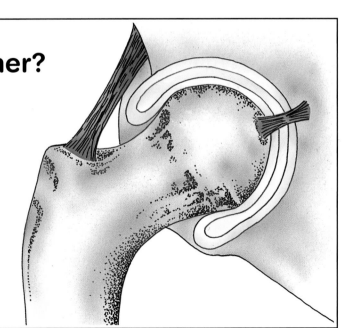

14

Find out more by looking
at pages **10–11**
20–21
22–23

On the move

Your body moves in many different ways. You can bend, stretch, turn, and twist. You can move because your bones move at your **joints**, places where your bones meet. But your bones can't move by themselves—they need something to pull at them. This job is done by your muscles, which are joined to your bones in order to move them.

Joints

There are many joints that help your body move. When you turn your head, bend your knees, or twist your wrists, your joints are in action. Some joints, such as those in your skull, do not move. These are called **fixed joints.** Each of the other kinds of joints does a specific type of movement.

Different kinds of joints

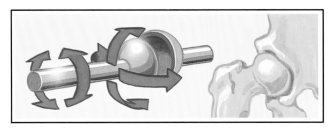

Ball and socket joints give you the most movement. The round end of one bone fits into a hollow part of another bone. Examples are your hip joints and shoulder joints.

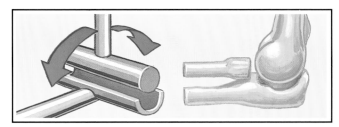

Hinge joints work like a door on a hinge. Movement in hinge joints is only in two directions. Your knees and elbows have hinge joints.

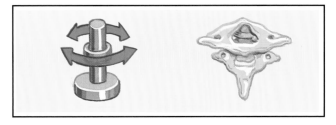

Pivot joints allow parts of your body to twist. Your head moves from side to side because it rests on a pivot joint at the top of your spine. In the same way, you can turn your hands over by flipping your wrists.

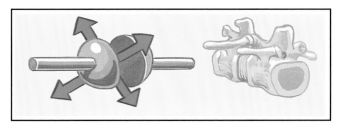

Gliding joints are one of the simplest kinds of joints. They allow a sliding movement when two pieces of bone come together. There are gliding joints on your backbone where the ribs meet the vertebrae.

Different kinds of muscle

There are more than 600 major muscles in your body. Not all are joined to your bones. For example, muscles line your blood vessels to keep blood flowing. Your lungs work because of regular muscle movement.

Some muscles move only when you decide to stand up, sit down, or move in other ways. These are the **voluntary muscles** that are joined to your bones. There are other muscles that work without your thinking about them. These **involuntary muscles** are made of smooth muscle fibers. They mash the food material in your stomach and then act to move it along through your intestines. Your heart is made of another special kind of muscle called **cardiac muscle**. It moves in a regular rhythm as it pumps blood to all parts of your body.

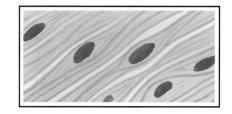

Smooth muscle is found in the stomach, in the intestines, and in the walls of blood vessels.

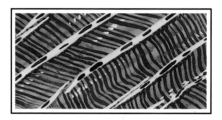

Striped muscles are the muscles that make your body move. They are attached to the bones.

How do muscles work?

Muscles are made of tough, elastic tissue. They are built so that they can **contract**, which means that they become shorter. When the muscles whose ends are joined to bones contract, they pull at the bones and make them move.

Muscles are made up of long, thin cells that join together to make muscle fibers. When the muscle becomes shorter, all the fibers move closer together, making the muscle bulge. You can see your muscles bulging and relaxing when you move your arms and legs. If you bend your elbow and clench your fist, the muscles called **biceps** in your upper arm will bulge.

Muscles can only pull—they can't push. Muscles whose ends are joined to bones work in pairs. One muscle contracts and pulls the bone one way, and the other contracts to pull the bone back again.

When you tighten your biceps muscle, you bend your arm. When the other big muscle in your arm, the triceps, tightens, your arm straightens out again.

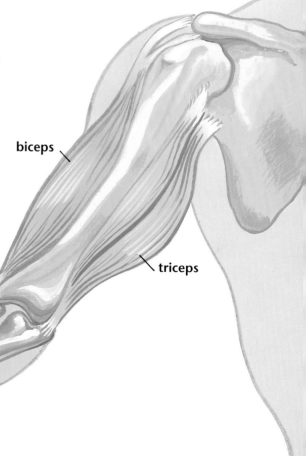

biceps

triceps

Find out more by looking at pages **18–19**

In and out

As you breathe, your chest moves in and out, and up and down. Inside your chest, there are two flexible, spongelike organs on either side of your heart. These are your **lungs**. When we **inhale** (take in air), we breathe in **oxygen**, a gas that helps to give us energy. When we **exhale** (expel air), we breathe out **carbon dioxide**, a harmful waste gas.

When you breathe in, your lungs fill with air and become larger. When you breathe out, your lungs become smaller as gas is squeezed out of them.

You breathe air in through your mouth and nose so that you can take in the oxygen your body needs.

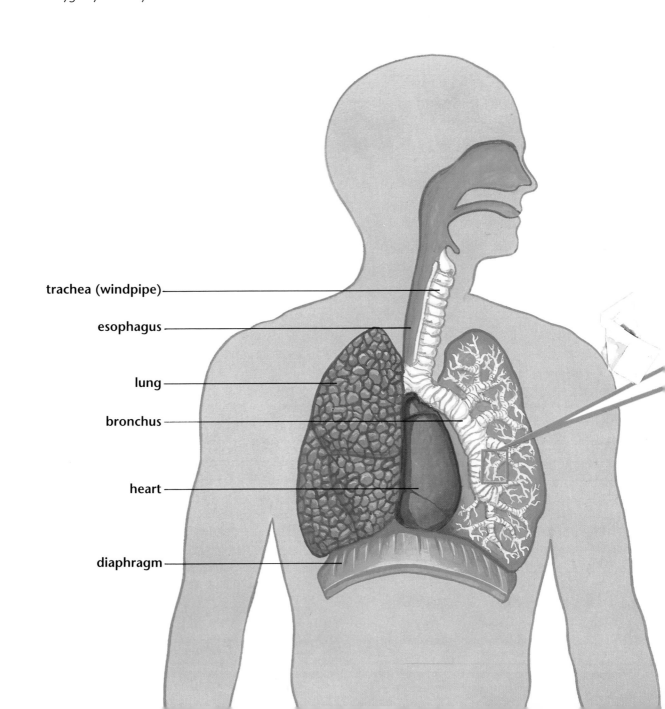

trachea (windpipe)

esophagus

lung

bronchus

heart

diaphragm

Breathing in

You inhale air through your nose and mouth. Inside your nose are tiny hairs that catch dust from the air. There is also a sticky liquid called **mucus** that warms and moistens the incoming air and catches many of the germs you breathe in.

The air you breathe in goes down a pipe called the **trachea**, also known as your windpipe. From your windpipe, air enters each lung through two tubes called **bronchi.** Each bronchus divides into smaller and smaller tubes, which eventually lead to tiny, elastic sacs called **alveoli.** There are many millions of alveoli in each lung. When air enters the alveoli, they blow up like tiny balloons. Then oxygen from the air passes through the walls of the alveoli into **capillaries**, which are very tiny tubelike vessels through which blood flows.

Breathing out

At the same time that oxygen enters your blood, waste gas passes from the blood into the alveoli. The air you exhale contains less oxygen and more carbon dioxide. This is the waste gas your body produces as oxygen breaks apart the chemicals in your food.

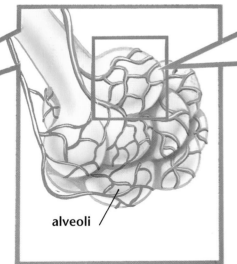

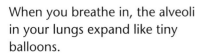
alveoli

When you breathe in, the alveoli in your lungs expand like tiny balloons.

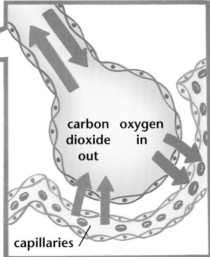
carbon dioxide out
oxygen in
capillaries

Oxygen passes into your capillaries. At the same time, carbon dioxide is passed out.

How you breathe

You have muscles in your chest that make you breathe. Some are fixed to your ribs and make your ribcage move in and out. Below your lungs is a strong, flat sheet of muscle called the **diaphragm.**

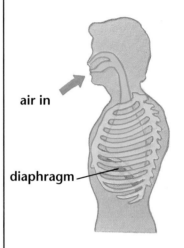
air in
diaphragm

As you breathe in, your diaphragm moves downward and your ribcage moves out, or expands. This makes a bigger space for the air that enters your lungs.

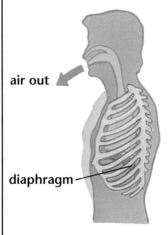
air out
diaphragm

As you breathe out, your ribcage and diaphragm squeeze your lungs into a smaller space again.

Around and around

Your blood has lots of different jobs to do as it travels around your body. It carries the oxygen you have breathed in to every single cell. It also carries food and other substances that your cells need. When the cells have done their job, they make waste products that your blood carries away.

What is blood made of?

Like other parts of your body, your blood is made from cells. There are two main kinds of blood cells—red and white. The **red blood cells** are the ones that contain a red substance called **hemoglobin.** It is the hemoglobin in the red blood cells that carries oxygen from the lungs. The **white blood cells** kill germs that enter your body. There are fewer white cells than red cells.

A liquid called **plasma** surrounds the blood cells. This is made mostly of water. The plasma carries food to the cells and carries waste products away.

The tubes that carry blood

Blood travels through tubes called **blood vessels.** The vessels that carry oxygen-rich blood away from your heart are called **arteries.** The vessels that return the blood to your heart are called **veins.** There are thousands of arteries and veins all over your body. They branch into a network of very tiny, tubelike blood vessels called capillaries. These are very thin so that they can carry blood to all the cells of your body.

Inside your veins are tiny flaps called **valves.** These open as blood is pushed through after each heartbeat, and they close again to stop the blood from running backwards.

These blood cells came from human blood. The two white blood cells in the middle help to fight germs.

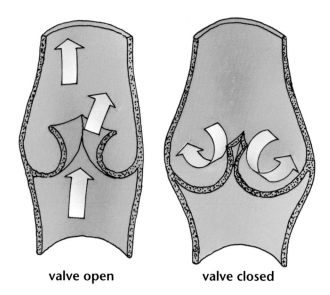

valve open   valve closed

Inside a vein, a valve opens as the blood flows through. The valve then closes to keep the blood from flowing back.

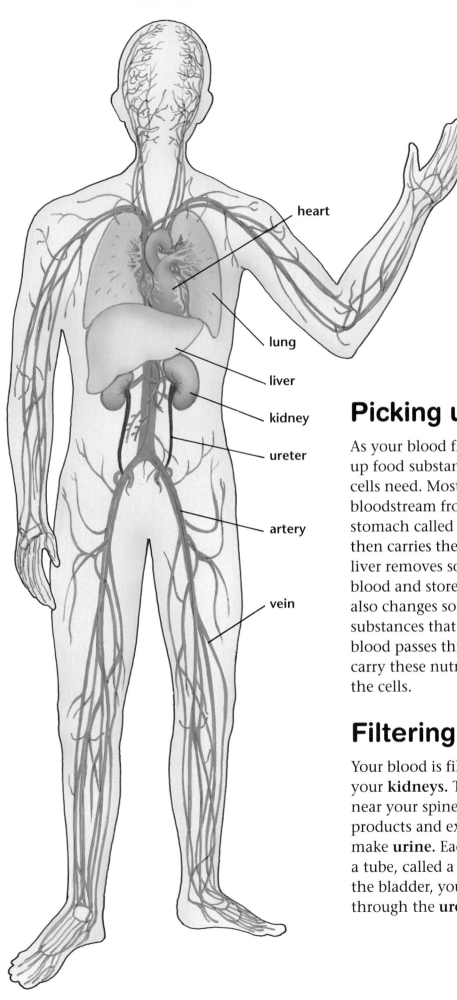

heart

lung

liver

kidney

ureter

artery

vein

Find out more by looking
at pages **20–21**
24–25

*Your heart is a strong muscle. It pumps
blood to all the different parts of your
body.*

Picking up food

As your blood flows through your body, it picks
up food substances, called **nutrients,** that your
cells need. Most of the nutrients enter your
bloodstream from an organ below your
stomach called the **small intestine.** Your blood
then carries the nutrients to your **liver.** Your
liver removes some of the nutrients from the
blood and stores them until they are needed. It
also changes some of the nutrients into other
substances that your body uses. After your
blood passes through your liver, it continues to
carry these nutrients and other substances to all
the cells.

Filtering the blood

Your blood is filtered when it passes through
your **kidneys.** These lie behind your stomach,
near your spine. They filter out some waste
products and extra salts from your blood and
make **urine.** Each kidney passes urine through
a tube, called a **ureter,** to your **bladder.** From
the bladder, you excrete urine every day
through the **urethra.**

Find out more by looking at pages **16–17**
18–19

Your heart

Your heart acts like a pump that's always working. It's made of strong muscle and is about the size of your fist. As it beats, it pumps blood to all the different parts of your body.

Blood from your heart carries oxygen that you breathe into your lungs to all the millions of cells in your body. Your body cells need oxygen to carry out their work and keep you alive.

How does your heart work?

Your heart has two main pumping parts that have different jobs to do. The left part pumps blood very strongly through the arteries of your body. This blood contains fresh oxygen from your lungs. The right part of your heart takes in blood returning from the veins of your body. This blood contains carbon dioxide, which is the waste gas that your cells give out as they use up oxygen. This blood is then pumped to your lungs, where carbon dioxide is exchanged for oxygen. The blood containing this fresh oxygen then continues to flow into the left part of your heart, from where it is pumped around your body once again.

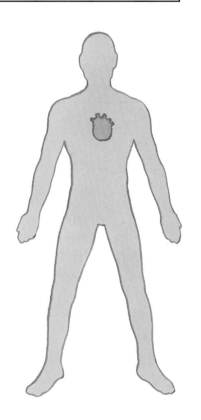

Your heart lies in your chest cavity, a little to the left of center.

Valves in each part of your heart open and shut in a way that prevents blood from flowing backward.

Faster and slower

After you have been running, your heart beats faster and you breathe more quickly. Why does this happen? The amount of carbon dioxide in your blood increases when you have been exercising. The rate and depth of your breathing increase to take the carbon dioxide out of your body. At the same time, the amount of oxygen you take in is increased.

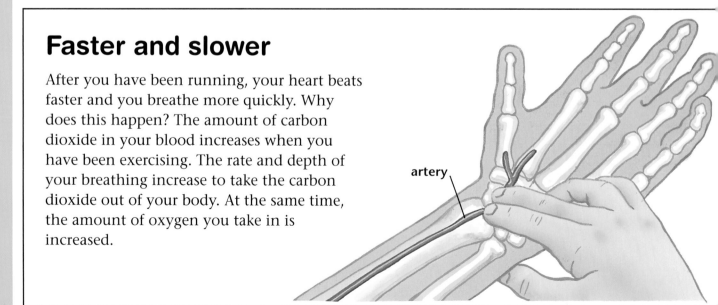

artery

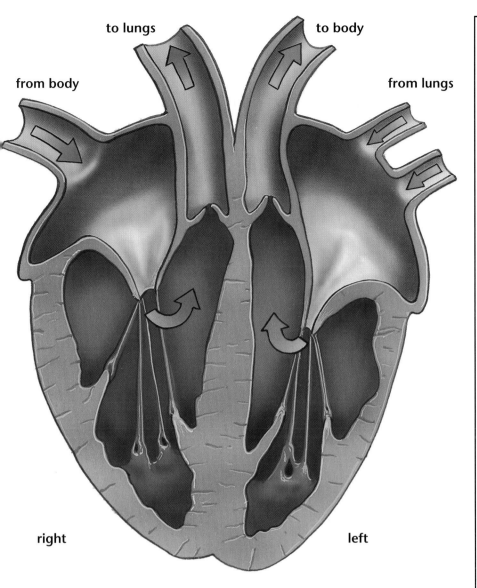

to lungs

to body

from body

from lungs

right

left

Speed up your pulse

1. Using a watch or clock with a second hand, count how many times your pulse beats in 30 seconds. Double the result to get your heart rate.

2. Then do some kind of exercise, such as jumping rope or skipping, for a few minutes.

3. Count your pulse beats again. How many are there in 30 seconds now? What is your heart rate?

Your **pulse** shows how fast your heart is beating. Every time your heart beats, blood surges through the artery in your wrist. If you put two fingers of one hand on the wrist of your other hand, you should feel a gentle and regular throbbing. This is your pulse. Use two fingers as shown.

You can feel your pulse at any point where an artery is near the surface of your skin.

Find out more by looking at page **60**

Where does your food go?

When you eat, your food begins a long journey through your body. Most of your food is broken down into lots of tiny, simple pieces so that your body can use it. This breaking-down process starts in your mouth and is called **digestion.** The various substances that aid in digestion are known as **digestive juices.**

Your body uses food to acquire energy. Food contains special chemicals that provide energy in your body's cells. Energy keeps all the different parts of your body working. Without energy, all your muscles and every other part of you would stop working. Food also helps your body grow and repair parts that have become worn out or damaged.

Food to keep you healthy

Food contains many different substances that work together to keep you going. Food substances that give you energy are called **carbohydrates** and **fats.** Carbohydrates are found in foods like potatoes, rice, and bread. Milk, butter, and cheese are fatty foods. The parts of your food that help your body grow and mend itself are called **proteins.** These are mainly found in meat, milk, eggs, nuts, and grain.

Your food also contains **vitamins** and **minerals,** which help you stay healthy. They make the chemicals in your body work properly. Food also contains tough parts called **fiber.** Fiber helps to keep your intestines in good working order. We take in water from our food, and from what we drink. Your blood needs a great deal of water to carry all these substances around your body.

2. After you have swallowed the food, it passes into your stomach, where a strong acid breaks it down. This process is helped by special chemicals called **enzymes.** There are lots of muscles in the stomach wall that mix the food up with digestive juices. The stomach acid also helps to kill germs in your food.

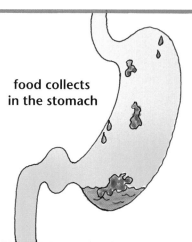

food collects in the stomach

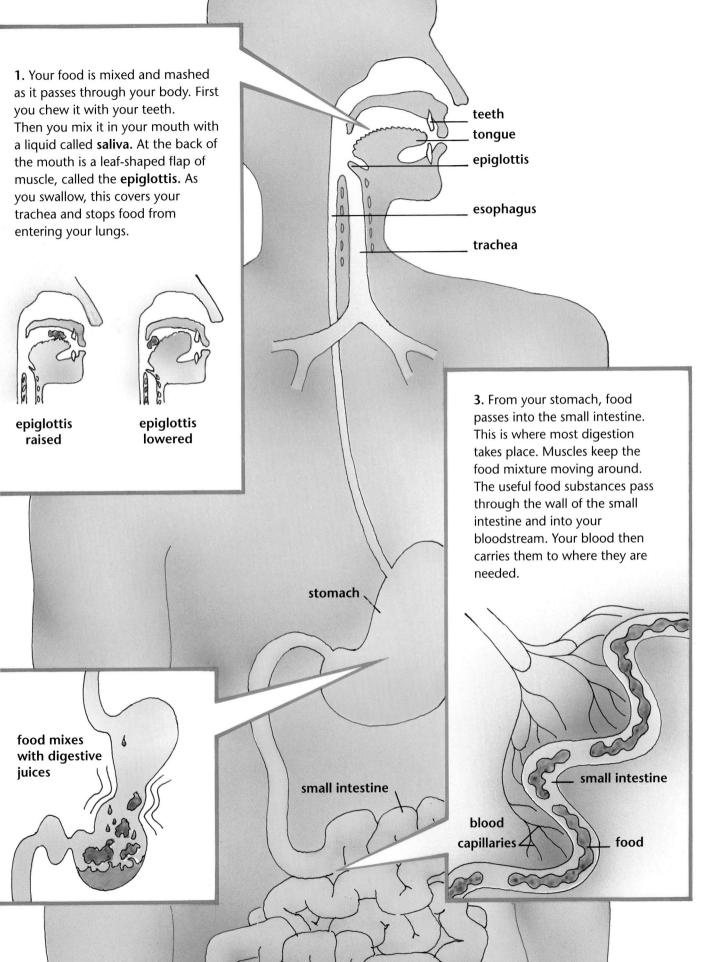

1. Your food is mixed and mashed as it passes through your body. First you chew it with your teeth. Then you mix it in your mouth with a liquid called **saliva.** At the back of the mouth is a leaf-shaped flap of muscle, called the **epiglottis.** As you swallow, this covers your trachea and stops food from entering your lungs.

epiglottis raised

epiglottis lowered

teeth

tongue

epiglottis

esophagus

trachea

3. From your stomach, food passes into the small intestine. This is where most digestion takes place. Muscles keep the food mixture moving around. The useful food substances pass through the wall of the small intestine and into your bloodstream. Your blood then carries them to where they are needed.

stomach

food mixes with digestive juices

small intestine

blood capillaries

small intestine

food

Find out more by looking at pages **18–19**

24

Clearing away waste

To keep you healthy, your body clears away the waste materials it cannot use. You breathe out a waste gas called carbon dioxide from your lungs. Your body can't digest some food, such as tough plant fibers. So you get rid of them as solid waste. Your body gets rid of other substances as liquid waste.

Getting rid of solid waste

Below the small intestine is the **large intestine.** Most of the food that reaches the large intestine is waste. The large intestine takes in, or absorbs, most of the water and minerals from the food as the food travels through it. This leaves solid waste, called **feces,** which collects in the lower bowel, or intestine, before it passes out from your body through an opening called the **anus.**

What are your kidneys?

Your kidneys make the liquid waste your body has to get rid of. You have two kidneys, one on each side of your spine, behind your stomach. They are shaped like beans and are nearly as large as your heart.

Your kidneys filter your blood as it travels through them. They take out waste products that your blood has carried away from all the cells. One of the main waste products is called **urea.** This is made after your cells have broken down substances called proteins. Your kidneys also take away some salt and water from your blood if it contains too much of them. Your body must keep a balance of salt and water. Keeping this balance is the responsibility of the kidneys.

Your kidneys then get rid of the water and waste products by making droplets of a liquid called urine. The urine passes into your bladder through two tubes called ureters. Your bladder is a bag made of muscle, which stretches as it fills with urine. When you decide it's time to expel the urine, the bladder squeezes it out through a tube called the **urethra.**

Your lungs remove carbon dioxide from your blood. Your kidneys remove waste liquid as urine, and your anus removes waste solids as feces.

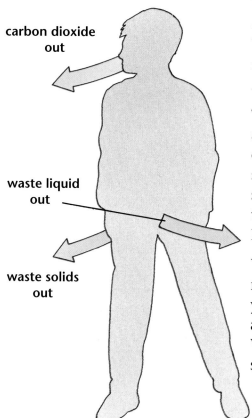

carbon dioxide
out

waste liquid
out

waste solids
out

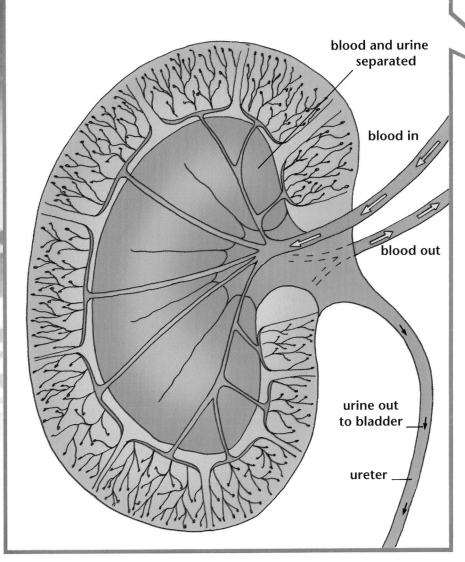

blood and urine
separated

blood in

blood out

urine out
to bladder

ureter

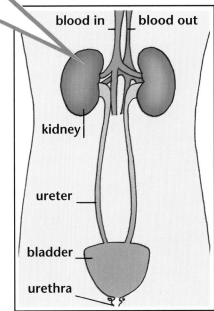

blood in   blood out

kidney

ureter

bladder

urethra

*Your kidneys remove waste
products from your blood. They
produce the urine that carries the
waste out of your body.*

Kidney machines

If your kidneys stop working
properly, dangerous waste
products stay in your blood.
A **kidney machine** can filter your
blood in the same way as a real
kidney. Blood from the patient's
body is pumped through a filter in
the machine. The filter takes out
the waste products. A second
pump returns blood back to the
patient.

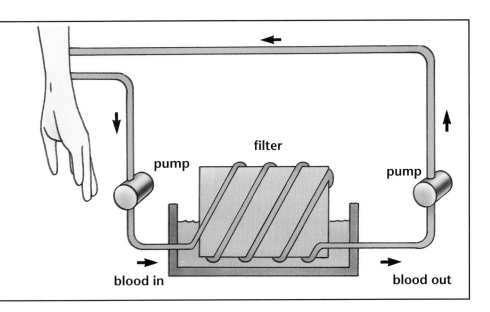

pump   filter   pump

blood in   blood out

Your senses

Can you name the five senses? Try to name them before reading further.

Sense organs are specially developed parts of your body. For example, each of your eyes has a retina for detecting light. And each of your ears has a cochlea for detecting sounds.

These senses send information to the brain. There are special parts in the brain that sort out this information. It is then passed to other parts of the brain, which can compare information from different sense organs. Your brain then signals what you are seeing, hearing, smelling, tasting, and touching. These five senses allow you to know what is in your physical environment.

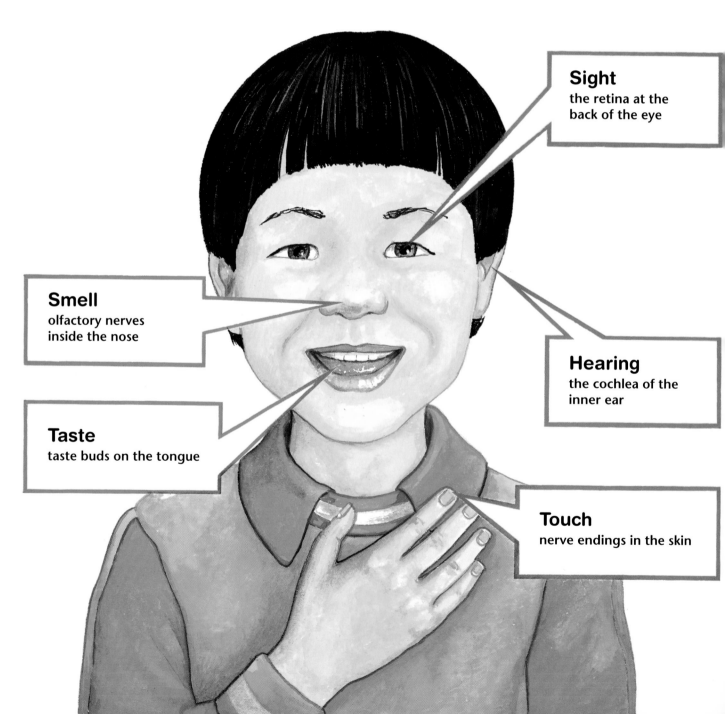

Sight
the retina at the back of the eye

Smell
olfactory nerves inside the nose

Hearing
the cochlea of the inner ear

Taste
taste buds on the tongue

Touch
nerve endings in the skin

The hidden senses

Another set of senses, which you are unaware of most of the time, helps control your inner organs. These senses control the timing and movement of food through your body. They measure the amount of sugar and salt in your blood. They regulate the amount of oxygen that's taken in. Your body temperature and the fullness of your bladder are also under the control of these senses. Without your awareness, your body is always receiving messages from your hidden senses. They keep all these basic processes, such as breathing and digestion, running smoothly.

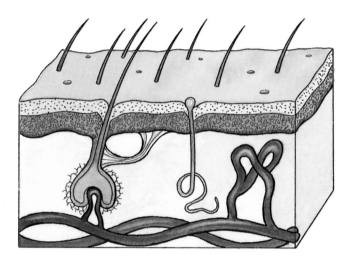

When you're hot, your skin produces droplets of sweat.

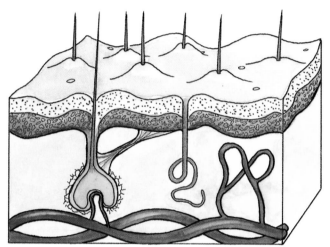

When you're cold, the hairs on your skin stand up.

A sense of time

Are you always late for everything? Or do you have a good "sense of time?" In fact, we all have a sense of time, often called our **biological clock**. It is something that we have in common with almost all animals. No one knows for certain what it is or how it works, but you are somehow aware when day changes into night, and night into day. During experiments, scientists have lived in deep, dark caves for periods of time. They found that, despite the darkness, their biological clock woke them up in the morning and made them slow down at night.

How do you hear?

Your ears aren't just flaps of skin on each side of your head. They are organs that stretch deep into the skull. They do a very important job. They collect sound waves, which are tiny vibrations of air, and change them into signals that your brain can understand.

To do the difficult job of hearing, the ear has three different parts. These are called the **outer ear**, the **middle ear**, and the **inner ear.**

The outer ear

The outer ear consists of the ear flap, which is the part you can see, and a hollow tube, called the **ear canal.** This leads to the **eardrum.** The eardrum is made of a sheet of skinlike material called a **membrane.** This vibrates when sound waves travel down the ear canal.

The middle ear

The middle ear is like a hollow cave. It contains three bones, called the **hammer,** the **anvil,** and the **stirrup.** When the eardrum vibrates, it makes the hammer vibrate. This movement is passed on to the anvil and then to the stirrup. The stirrup makes another membrane, called the **oval window,** vibrate.

The inner ear

Behind the oval window is the inner ear. This is made up of the **cochlea,** the **vestibule,** and the **semicircular canals.** The cochlea has three tubes, which are coiled like a snail's shell. These tubes are filled with fluid. When the oval window vibrates, it makes waves in the fluid. One of the tubes has thousands of sensitive hairs. When the fluid passes over the hairs, it prompts your nerves to carry messages about sound to your brain.

An acrobat needs to have a very good sense of balance to do a trick like this.

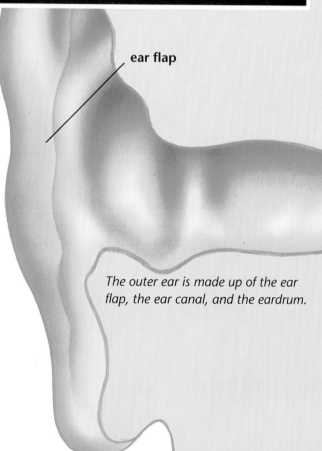

ear flap

The outer ear is made up of the ear flap, the ear canal, and the eardrum.

Keeping your balance

The semicircular canals help you keep your balance. They also contain fluid and sensitive hairs. If you tip your head to one side, the fluid in these tubes moves, and the sensitive hairs let the brain know what has happened.

The vestibule is a chamber between the canals and the cochlea. It contains two sacs, also filled with fluid and sensitive hair cells. The sacs have chalky particles inside them, which are pulled to Earth by the force of gravity. When you stand upright, the particles press on the hairs at the bottom of each sac. When you lie down, the particles settle to one side and press on a different set of hairs. Nerves from the hairs signal your brain about the position of your body.

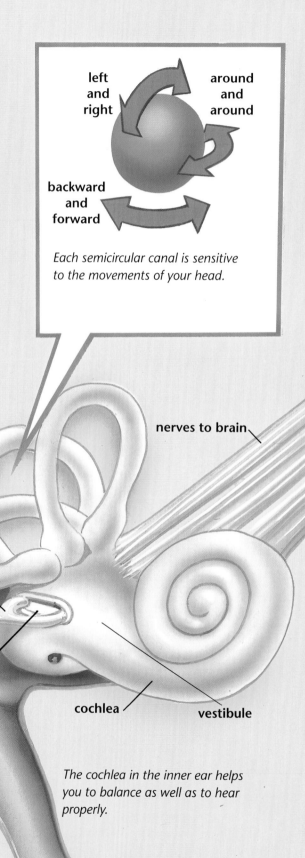

left and right

around and around

backward and forward

Each semicircular canal is sensitive to the movements of your head.

semicircular canals

stirrup

anvil

hammer

ear canal

nerves to brain

eardrum

oval window

tube to throat

cochlea

vestibule

The middle ear contains three tiny bones—the hammer, the anvil, and the stirrup.

The cochlea in the inner ear helps you to balance as well as to hear properly.

Taste and smell

Your tongue is your main taste organ. You also use your tongue to break up and swallow your food. Your tongue is covered with tiny spots called **taste buds.** They allow you to notice the difference between the four tastes—**sweet, salty, sour,** and **bitter.**

You will need:

five sheets of paper

a pencil

water

sugar

salt

vinegar or lemon juice

strong, unsweetened black tea or coffee

paper tissues

four saucers

4 glass or plastic droppers, or 4 small teaspoons

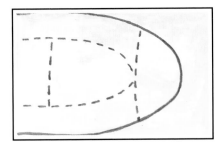

6. Now you are ready to map a tongue! On a sheet of paper, draw an outline of a tongue that matches the one shown above.

7. Now divide the tongue up into five areas as pictured above.

Map your tongue

There are four areas on your tongue which pick up different tastes. Find them by making a map of the tongue.

1. First, label four of the sheets of paper as "sweet," "salty," "sour," and "bitter."

2. In one saucer, dissolve some sugar in water. Place this saucer on the paper marked "sweet."

3. In another saucer, dissolve some salt in water. Place this on the paper marked "salty."

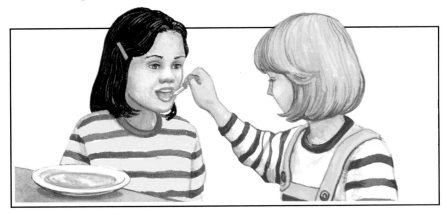

4. In a third saucer, mix the vinegar or lemon juice with an equal amount of water. Put this on the paper marked "sour."

5. Pour the tea into the last saucer. Place this on the paper marked "bitter."

8. Wash your hands well. Dry your friend's tongue with a plain paper towel and place a drop of the sweet liquid on the tip of the tongue. If your friend can taste the sweetness, mark that part of your map "sweet." Do the same for the other three liquids, using a new dropper or spoon for each type.

9. Now do the same for the other four areas of the tongue, but test the liquids in a different order each time.

What does your tongue map show? Does each area of the tongue pick up a different taste?

A sense of smell

Smells are really chemicals floating about in the air. Your nose has special parts called **receptors** that respond to these smells. If a chemical appears, a receptor sends a message along the nerves to your brain. Your brain translates this message into a sensation of a "nice" or a "nasty" smell. Your nose is sensitive to different kinds of chemicals, but it can't interpret them.

Smell is important to us because it helps our sense of taste. Your tongue can only pick up the four basic tastes—sweet, salty, sour, and bitter. It's your nose that makes tomatoes taste like tomatoes and apples taste like apples. Without a sense of smell, they would taste much the same.

Find out more by looking at pages **40–41**

You will need:

a knife

a blindfold

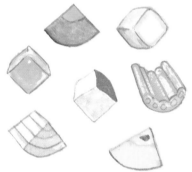

some foods, such as apple, celery, melon, potato, carrot, and onion

Hold your nose!

You can test the sense of smell by feeding different foods to a friend who is blindfolded while holding his or her nose. All the foods should have about the same texture.

1. Wash your hands well with soap and water. Then cut up the foods into pieces. Blindfold your friend and make sure your friend is holding his or her nose.

2. Now feed each of these foods in turn to your friend. Give the onion last. Otherwise its strong taste might spoil the other tastes. Can your friend tell you what the different foods are?

3. Now ask your friend to try each food again, but hold another type of food under your friend's nose at the same time. What happens?

Find out more by looking at pages **40–41**

Your outer covering

Your skin protects your body. It keeps out dirt, rain, and wind. It also has many other jobs to do. In your skin, there are nerves that sense pain, temperature, and pressure. These nerves act as sensors and send messages to your brain. They give you your sense of touch.

Touching gives you different kinds of sensations. Close your eyes and run your fingers over some objects around you. Describe what your fingertips are feeling.

You will need:

hot water

cold water

three glass jars

Hot and cold

Does your body feel temperature changes as accurately as a thermometer? Find out by following this experiment.

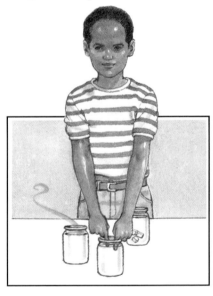

1. Fill one jar with hot tap water, not too hot to put your finger in. Fill the other jar with cold water, or iced water if available. In the third jar, make a mixture of the two.

Remember that even hot tap water can scald!

2. Place the forefinger of one hand into the jar of hot water and the forefinger of your other hand into the jar of cold water. Leave them there for a few minutes.

3. Now take both fingers out, and immediately put them into the third jar. What are your fingers telling you about the temperature of the water? Are they saying the same thing?

Your skin does not measure temperature as accurately as a thermometer, does it? Your estimation of temperature depends on how hot or cold your skin is to begin with.

Beneath your skin

The skin on your body has three layers. The top layer is called the **epidermis**. It contains four layers of cells. The next layer of skin is called the **dermis**. Your nerves are found here. It also contains small tissues called **glands**. These produce a liquid called **sweat** and another substance which oils the hairs and skin. The **fatty layer** is the deepest layer. In all people it varies in thickness.

Sweating it out

When we get too hot, our bodies are in danger. Many parts of our bodies will work properly only if the temperature inside is just right—about 98.6 °F (37 °C). In particular, the vital chemicals called **enzymes** are of no use if the temperature is too high or too low. Some way of cooling high body temperature is necessary to maintain a fairly constant temperature.

The main way that we cool down is by producing sweat. This liquid oozes out of the **pores** in our skin whenever the body temperature is too high. When this liquid evaporates, it takes away heat, causing the body to "cool down." **Evaporation** of sweat from the skin's surface is thus a cooling process.

New skin cells grow at the bottom of the epidermis all the time. They push older cells gradually to the surface, where they flake off.

hair

top of epidermis   pore

bottom of epidermis

cell sensitive to temperature

oily gland

dermis

nerve sensitive to touch

muscle

blood vessel

sweat gland

fatty layer

nerve

The amazing eye

Your eyes are like two tiny movie cameras inside your head. They are sending a steady stream of pictures back to your brain, like a television camera sending live pictures back to a TV screen.

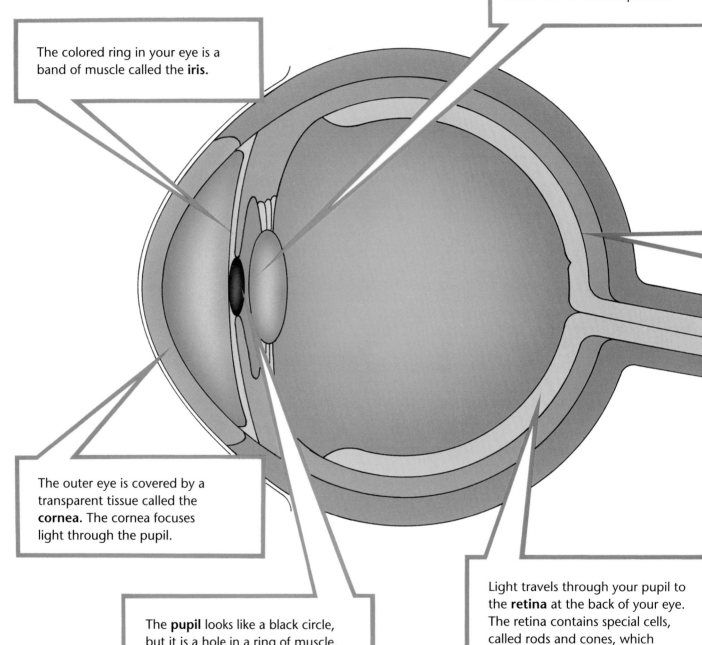

Your eyes have a part called the **lens,** just like a camera. The lens helps to bring everything you look at into focus, so that details are as clear as possible.

The colored ring in your eye is a band of muscle called the **iris.**

The outer eye is covered by a transparent tissue called the **cornea.** The cornea focuses light through the pupil.

The **pupil** looks like a black circle, but it is a hole in a ring of muscle. The pupil opens up to let in more light when it is dark and closes in the presence of bright light.

Light travels through your pupil to the **retina** at the back of your eye. The retina contains special cells, called rods and cones, which respond to light and color. Nerves carry messages from these cells to your brain.

Rods and cones

Human beings, unlike many other animals, can see in color. Some other animals, such as birds and butterflies, can also see colors.

To see colors, we have special cells in the eye called **cones.** They share the work of seeing with other cells called **rods.** Rods do not detect the difference between colors and don't need as much light as cones to make them work. So at times, rods are more useful to you than cones, such as at night when the light is very dim.

Have you ever been for a walk in the moonlight and noticed how pale, silvery, and colorless everything seems? Photographers can take pictures by moonlight that are just as colorful as pictures taken by day. So the colors are still there by moonlight, but we can't see them. Can you think why this is?

The cones help us to see color, but moonlight doesn't provide them with enough light to function well at night.

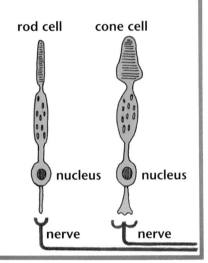

The rods and cones in your retina absorb the light that enters your eye. They pass messages about the light through nerves to your brain.

rod cell   cone cell

nucleus   nucleus

nerve   nerve

Changing shape

Muscles pull on the lens to change its shape. This allows you to look at something far away and then to focus on an object close by. As you look from the faraway object to the nearby one, your lens changes shape. A sharp picture of the object is focused onto the back of the inside of your eyeball. When you look back at the faraway scene, the lens changes back to its original shape so quickly that you don't even notice.

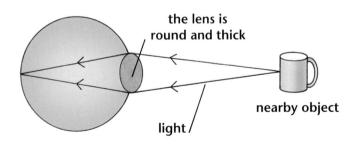

the lens is round and thick

nearby object

light

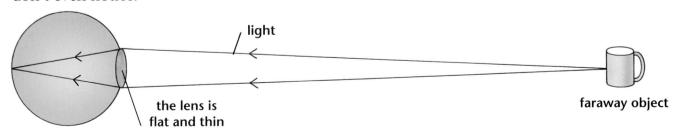

light

the lens is flat and thin

faraway object

Find out more by looking at pages **34–35**

Different animals have their eyes in different positions.

Why do we have two eyes?

Look at the pictures of the woodcock and the boy on this page. What do you notice about the position of their eyes?

Why do you think the woodcock has its eyes on the sides of its head? If you watch a woodcock feeding, you will see why. The woodcock has to keep a constant lookout for enemies such as foxes, so it needs to be able to see all around. In fact, many birds can see all around them, to help protect them from danger.

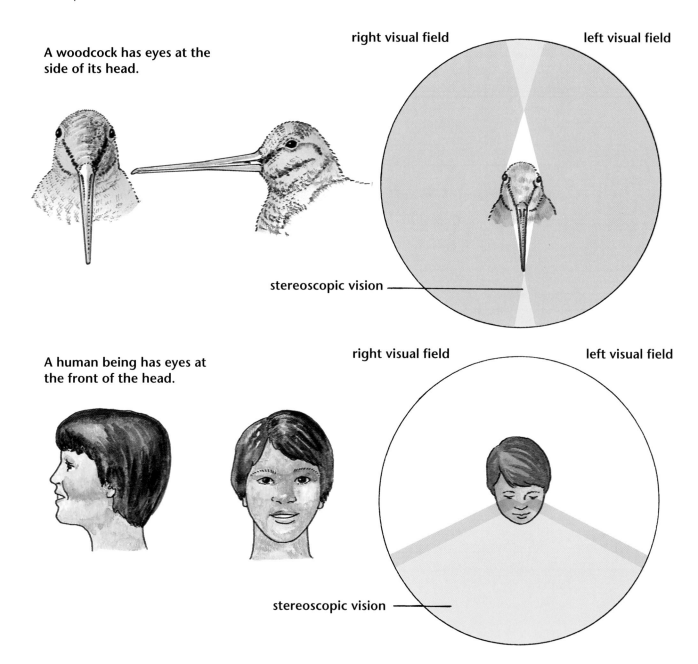

A woodcock has eyes at the side of its head.

right visual field   left visual field

stereoscopic vision

A human being has eyes at the front of the head.

right visual field   left visual field

stereoscopic vision

You will need:

stiff, black paper or cloth

scissors

a sharp pencil

a ball

thin elastic or ribbon

Two eyes see better than one

Why are our eyes on the front of our head, both looking the same way? It seems a waste of an eye, but maybe not. To find out how your two eyes work together, play this game of throwing and catching a ball with a friend.

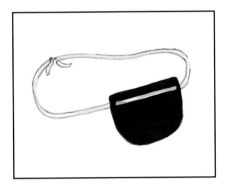

1. Cut out an eyepatch from the paper or cloth. Using the pencil point, make a small hole on each side of the patch. Thread the elastic or ribbon through the patch.

2. Using both eyes, play at catching the ball. Throw the ball 20 times, and make a record of how often you drop the ball.

3. Now cover one eye with your patch. Keep a record for another 20 catches. Did you do as well? Explain what happened.

Stereoscopic vision

When we use both our eyes, we have a kind of sight called **stereoscopic vision.** Because both eyes are at the front, they both see the same object. But your eyes are a little apart from each other, so each has a slightly different view of things. You can check this if you place two objects, such as drinking glasses, on a table in front of you. Place one about 8 inches (20 centimeters) away from you, the other 2 feet (60 centimeters) away. Put your chin on the table with the two glasses in a straight line away from you. Close one eye, then the other. Do you see exactly the same thing with both eyes?

Your brain makes use of the fact that your eyes tell different stories. By comparing the messages from each eye, your brain figures out how far away an object is. Your brain does this in a split second every time you look at anything.

Find out more by looking at pages **36–37**

Children may take several years to develop good coordination. They learn to coordinate their hands and eyes when doing simple things, such as balancing blocks on top of one another.

Coordinating your body

Your brain is a most remarkable organ! It sends out and receives hundreds of messages every second of your life. Your brain controls your muscles, sense organs, temperature—even your appetite! Your brain is also the place where thinking and remembering happen.

Your brain plays a very important part in your body's **coordination.** It controls the messages from your muscles and sense organs. When you stand on your toes, your brain receives messages from your eyes, ears, and joints about the position of your body. At the same time, your brain signals to your muscles what to do to keep your body balanced.

Is seeing always believing?

All you need for this experiment is a narrow cardboard tube or a sheet of paper rolled up to make a tube.

1. Look out of the window and hold the tube to your right eye. Close your left eye to check what your right eye is seeing.

Now open both eyes. What can you see? Explain what happens.

2. Still with both eyes open, hold your left hand up in front of you with your open palm toward your face. Lightly touching the tube with the side of your hand, slowly slide your hand back and forth until you see a hole in the middle of the palm. What can you see through the hole?

3. Still holding the tube to your eye, hold a finger up next to the tube. Is there a hole in your finger? Can you explain the difference?

Your brain figures it out

When you held up your hand, the part of your brain that receives information from your eyes became confused. It had to match up two completely different views coming from your eyes. It matched these views by showing your hand with a hole in the middle that framed the view through the tube. When you were just holding up a finger, it could sort out the two views because the finger did not blot out the view through the tube completely. So it did not need to make a hole in the finger.

This experiment shows you something even more important about your brain. You never thought that your hand really had a hole in it. Another part of your brain told you that information from your eyes was incorrect. So your brain has a special part that makes sense of confusing information.

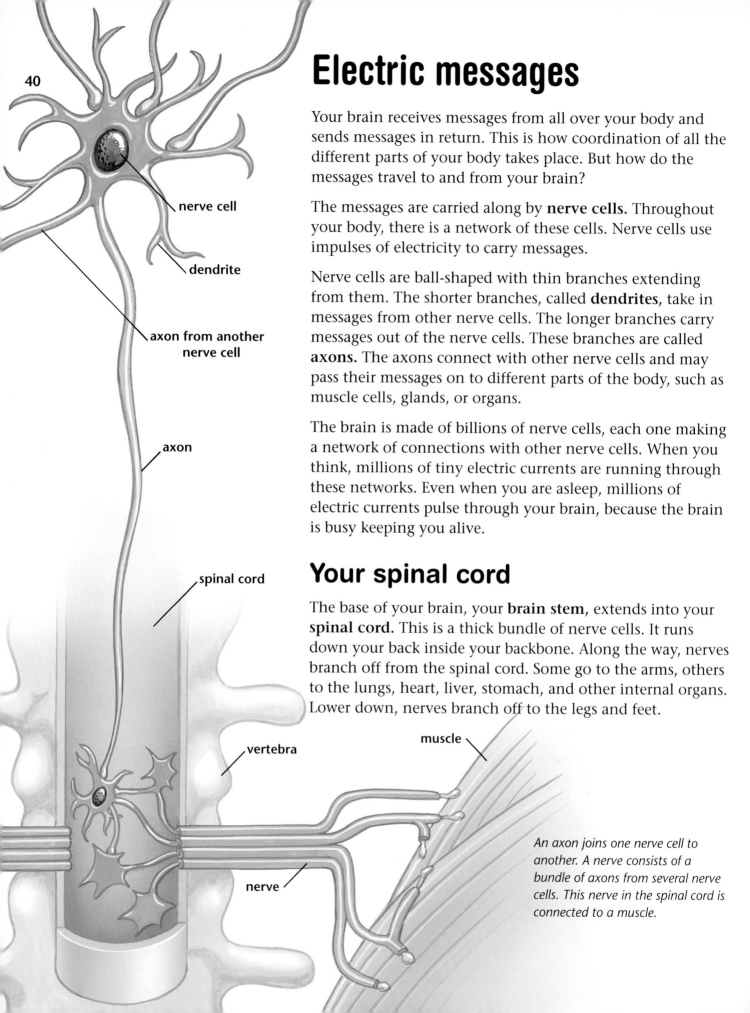

nerve cell

dendrite

axon from another
nerve cell

axon

spinal cord

vertebra

nerve

Electric messages

Your brain receives messages from all over your body and sends messages in return. This is how coordination of all the different parts of your body takes place. But how do the messages travel to and from your brain?

The messages are carried along by **nerve cells.** Throughout your body, there is a network of these cells. Nerve cells use impulses of electricity to carry messages.

Nerve cells are ball-shaped with thin branches extending from them. The shorter branches, called **dendrites,** take in messages from other nerve cells. The longer branches carry messages out of the nerve cells. These branches are called **axons.** The axons connect with other nerve cells and may pass their messages on to different parts of the body, such as muscle cells, glands, or organs.

The brain is made of billions of nerve cells, each one making a network of connections with other nerve cells. When you think, millions of tiny electric currents are running through these networks. Even when you are asleep, millions of electric currents pulse through your brain, because the brain is busy keeping you alive.

Your spinal cord

The base of your brain, your **brain stem,** extends into your **spinal cord.** This is a thick bundle of nerve cells. It runs down your back inside your backbone. Along the way, nerves branch off from the spinal cord. Some go to the arms, others to the lungs, heart, liver, stomach, and other internal organs. Lower down, nerves branch off to the legs and feet.

muscle

An axon joins one nerve cell to another. A nerve consists of a bundle of axons from several nerve cells. This nerve in the spinal cord is connected to a muscle.

Reflex movements

Your leg muscles flex and move to allow you to stand up because your brain has sent them messages on what to do. But there are some movements, such as pulling your hand away from something hot, that do not involve the brain. These are called **reflexes.** Reflexes help to protect you from danger. Blinking your eyes as something comes very close to your face is another reflex.

Doctors can test whether your reflexes are working properly by using the knee-jerk test. You sit on a chair with one leg crossed over the other. The doctor taps a spot just below the knee of the top leg, and your leg jerks into the air. You can't control it. When your knee is tapped, a message travels up a nerve in your thigh to your spinal cord. It does not go to the brain. The spinal cord sends a message straight back to a nerve connected to the thigh muscle. This muscle contracts suddenly and your leg jerks upward.

41

Find out more by looking at pages **34–35**
38–39

It takes a very short time for the knee-jerk message to travel to your spinal cord and back to your muscle —only about one-twentieth of a second.

doctor taps your knee here

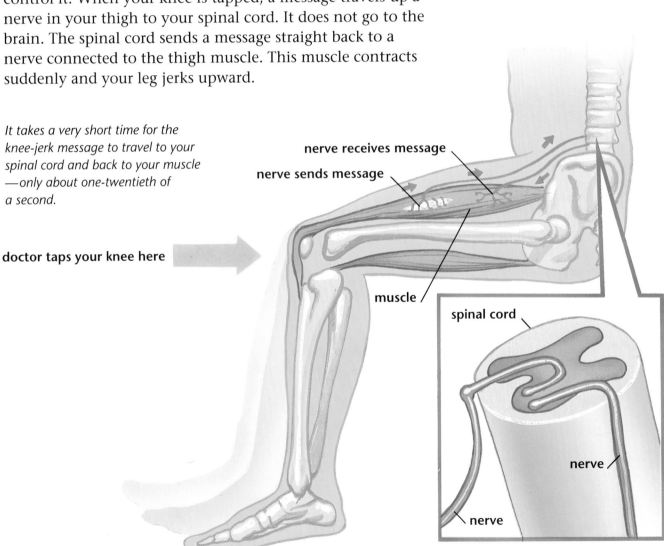

nerve receives message

nerve sends message

muscle

spinal cord

nerve

nerve

Controlling movement

You have discovered that your brain is responsible for coordinating many of your body's movements. These movements can be directly controlled by you—unlike reflexes that do not involve the brain. But these movements do not always come naturally. Often, they have to be learned. If you want to ride a bicycle, you must learn to pedal, to balance, and to lean to one side when you ride around a corner.

You will need:

a long ruler

paper

a felt-tipped pen

Test the speed of your reactions

In these tests, you can find out about the speed of your sense of sight and sense of touch. In both these tests, hold your thumb and forefinger so that they are just touching the ruler. For the sight test, watch the ruler to see when it falls and grab it as quickly as possible. For the touch test, close your eyes and grab the ruler as soon as you feel it falling.

Do some sight tests and some touch tests. Then make separate record sheets for each test. Record the distances measured on the ruler for every test you do. Ask a friend to help you.

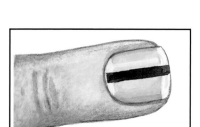

1. First, ask your friend to draw a line on your thumbnail with the pen. This is lined up with the line marked "O" on the ruler each time the test is performed.

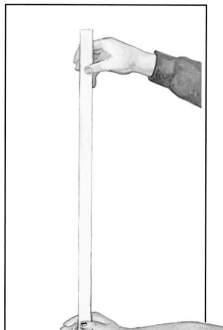

2. Ask your friend to hold the ruler between the thumb and forefinger, then to drop it without any warning. You must try to catch the ruler by closing your thumb and forefinger together as quickly as you can.

3. Use the lines on the ruler as a measure of how long it took you to react. Each time you catch the ruler, record the place where the thumbnail line is.

Which type of reaction is faster? What does this test show?

Learning actions

You can learn to make certain movements or actions by practicing them over and over again. When you get used to them, your brain helps you to do them almost automatically. Once a baby has learned to walk, for example, he or she will be able to walk without having to think about it. Though the act of walking is more or less automatic, the child can still choose to walk slowly or quickly.

These children have learned how to play their musical instruments by practicing regularly.

Practice makes perfect

Does a task you're not used to doing take longer than a task you are used to doing? Can you get better and quicker at the task by doing it again and again?

You will need:

three sheets of lined paper

a pencil

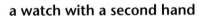

a watch with a second hand

1. Number the lines on a sheet of paper from 1 to 20.

2. Time yourself as you write out any word 20 times. You can write your name if you like. At the bottom of the page, write down how long it took.

3. Number 20 lines on the second sheet of paper.

4. Timing yourself again, write the word 20 times backwards. How long did this take?

5. On the third sheet of paper, write out the word backwards another 20 times. Has your speed improved?

Chemicals in charge

Are you tall for your age, or short? How tall you grow depends mostly on chemical substances called **hormones**, which move around your body in your blood.

Some hormones cause the cells in your body to make more protein. They then make the cells grow and divide, so that all of your body gets bigger. Because hormones are going around in your blood, they reach every cell in your body. So all your cells grow and divide. This is why hormones are so important. They control the different parts of your body, so that everything is regulated. Hormones are regulators of chemical and growth activity in the body.

This boy and this girl are both eight years old. How tall you grow depends mostly on hormones.

Linking with your brain

The balance of hormones in your blood is controlled by the **pituitary gland**, which lies just below the brain. The pituitary gland produces hormones that control many of the body's activities. Large numbers of nerve cells and blood vessels link the pituitary gland to a part of the brain called the **hypothalamus.** The hypothalamus controls the pituitary gland by sending "on" and "off" messages through the nerve cells and the bloodstream. These messages tell the pituitary gland when to start and stop releasing certain hormones.

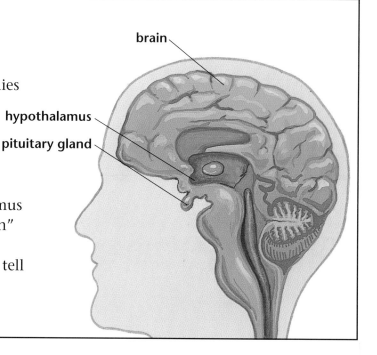

brain

hypothalamus

pituitary gland

Glands produce hormones

Most of your body's hormones are produced by **glands** that are known as **endocrine glands.** The hormones made by your pituitary gland control the production of hormones from some of the other glands.

The **pituitary gland** is the main hormone-producing gland. It lies just underneath your brain. The pituitary gland produces many different hormones, including the ones that control your growth and others that control your kidneys.

The **thyroid gland** lies in your neck, on either side of your trachea. It produces hormones that make your body processes go faster or slower.

The **adrenal glands** lie just above your kidneys. They produce hormones that control the amount of salts and **glucose** (a type of sugar) in your blood. They also produce **adrenalin,** which prepares your body for danger.

The **pancreas** produces the hormone **insulin,** which controls the amount of sugar in your blood. Its juices help you to digest your food.

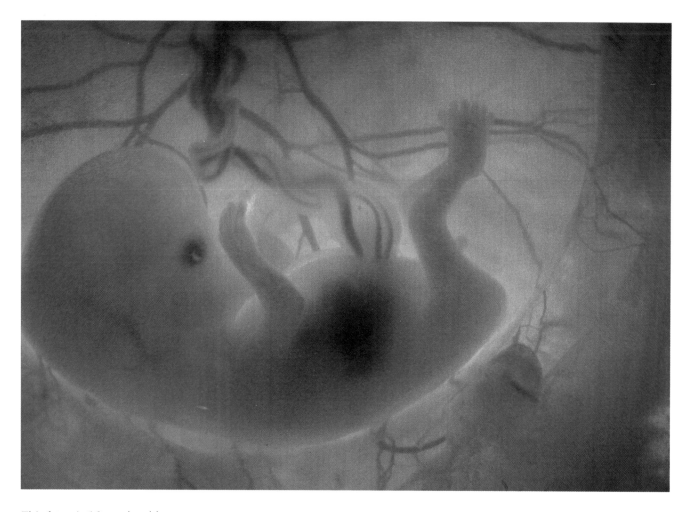

This fetus is 12 weeks old.

This fetus is 38 weeks old. The baby will soon be born.

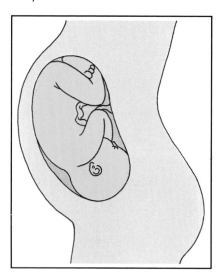

Where and how you began life

If you were a bird or a fish, you would have begun life by hatching out of an egg. Because you belong to a group of animals called mammals, you spent the first nine months of your life inside your mother. Human beings produce eggs, just as birds and fish do, but they are much smaller than the head of a pin. The mother keeps the fertilized egg inside her, so that her baby can grow protected from the outside world. Before the baby is born, it's called a **fetus.** The fetus grows inside a part of the mother called the **uterus,** or womb.

While you were growing inside your mother, you took in nourishment through a flexible tube called the **umbilical cord.** This was joined to a disk-shaped organ inside the uterus called the **placenta.** As your mother's blood flowed through the placenta, it supplied you with all the food and oxygen you needed.

Growing inside the womb

For nine months, you grew larger and slowly changed shape inside your mother's womb. Then the time came when you were ready to be born.

A mother carries the baby inside her body for nine months. During this period, the fetus grows and develops until it is ready to be born.

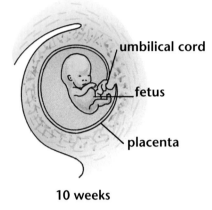

10 weeks

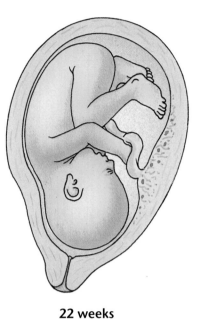

22 weeks

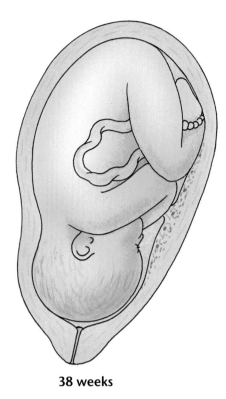

38 weeks

Being born

During your birth, strong muscles in your mother's womb squeezed you out into a passage called the **vagina.** From here, you came out into the world. Then the umbilical cord, which attached you to the placenta, was cut. Your belly button, called the **navel,** is where the cord was once attached to you. After you were born you continued to grow. Your body grows rapidly until you are between the ages of 12 and 17, then continues to grow more slowly until you reach your adult size by about the age of 23.

During birth, muscles inside the mother's womb push the baby out through the vagina.

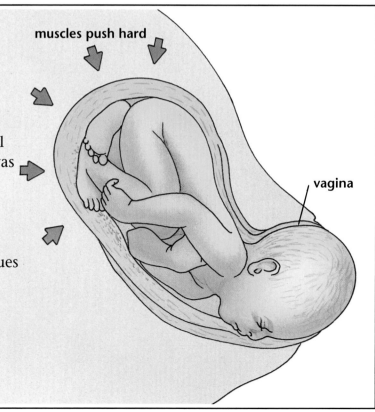

48

Find out more by looking
at pages **52–53**
56–57

What makes you ill?

You can get sick in various ways—from not eating a balanced diet to breathing in too many automobile fumes. You can also become ill by catching a disease. Many diseases are caused by small living things, such as **bacteria** and **viruses**, which can live inside your body. Often we call these things germs, but scientists call them **microorganisms**, or **microbes.** The microbes are always trying to attack you, and your body has to fight to stop them, or it becomes ill. Other living things called **protists** can cause disease, too. Larger creatures, such as worms and flukes, can also live inside people and make them ill.

These rod-shaped bacteria are on a human tooth. They are not really red but have been colored so that they are easier to see.

Bacteria

Bacteria are so small that you can see them only through a microscope. Certain bacteria cause diseases such as scarlet fever, salmonella food poisoning, cholera, and whooping cough. Bacteria in people's mouths can cause tooth decay. Many other kinds of bacteria live in your intestines or on your skin. These are harmless most of the time. But if your body isn't working properly, these bacteria may invade other parts and make you ill.

Viruses

Viruses are very small, much smaller than bacteria. They can't live on their own. They can reproduce only inside living cells of other bodies. Diseases caused by viruses include the common cold, influenza, measles, mumps, smallpox, yellow fever, and AIDS (Acquired Immunodeficiency Syndrome).

Microbes can get inside, or invade, our bodies in many ways. Some microbes can be caught from other people when they cough or sneeze into the air you are breathing.

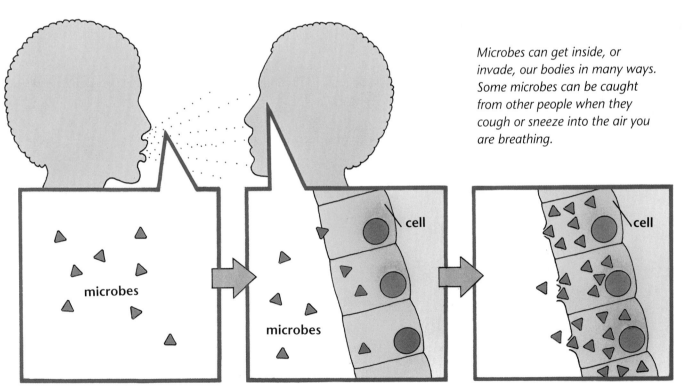

1. When people cough and sneeze, microbes are pushed out into the air.

2. When you breathe in the microbes, the germs have a new body to invade.

3. The microbes attack the cells in your body, making you ill.

Defending your body

Your body has a way of fighting germs to protect you from diseases. Inside your body, there are millions of cells that kill invading microbes, such as bacteria and viruses. These cells make up your **immune system**, which keeps you healthy most of the time.

Your body makes the cells of your immune system in bone marrow. Large concentrations of these cells are found in certain internal organs, like the lymph nodes, the spleen, and the liver.

Different kinds of cells make up your immune system. Some move around your body in your blood. These are white blood cells known as **lymphocytes**. When they find invading microbes, they pass through the walls of the blood vessels to attack them.

Eating cells

Some immune cells kill germs by simply eating them. These cells are called **phagocytes**, which means "eating cells." They are also known as **macrophages**. Chemicals called **antibodies** stick to the microbes so that the phagocytes know where they are. If the virus that causes measles gets into your body, you will start making antibodies that stick all over the surface of the virus, like a label. The phagocytes can then find the measles viruses and destroy them.

How do eating cells work?

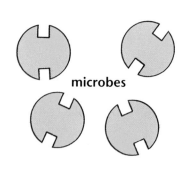

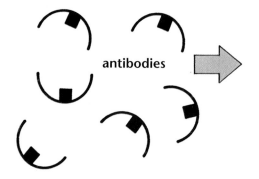

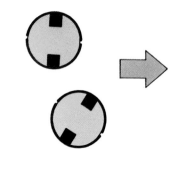

1. The microbes, such as bacteria or viruses, enter your body.

2. Your body makes special chemicals, called antibodies. These are released into the bloodstream.

3. An antibody recognizes a microbe and sticks to it.

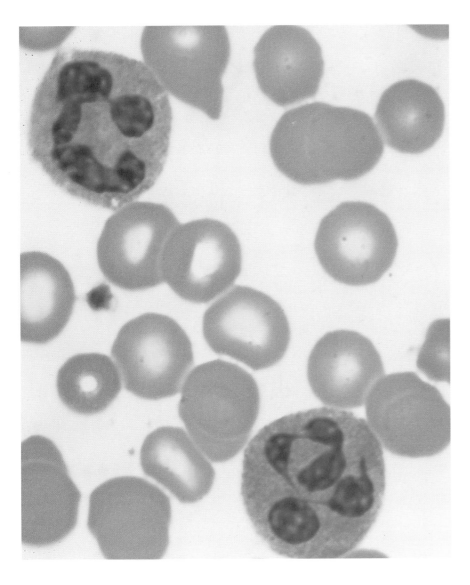

Your blood contains red cells and larger white cells. White blood cells are an important part of your body's immune system. They attack and destroy microbes that invade your body.

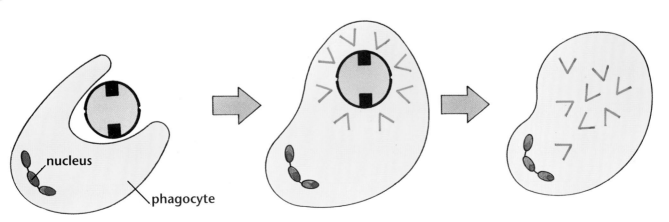

4. An eating cell, or phagocyte, starts to surround a microbe.

5. The phagocyte completely surrounds the microbe and digests it.

6. The microbe is destroyed, so the chance of getting sick is decreased.

Keeping disease away

Some diseases that are caused by viruses, such as cholera, will make you ill only once. How does your body stop you from having some diseases more than once?

The first time you have the virus, your body will take some time to make antibodies against it. That is why you are ill for a while. As soon as the antibodies start working, you begin to feel better. Once you are better, your body is repeatedly able to make the antibodies for that particular virus.

In the United States, vaccinations are an important part of preventive medicine for children.

If the virus enters your body again, your body can make antibodies much more quickly than the first time. The antibodies defeat the virus without your knowing about it. You are now **immune** to that virus, which means that your body can protect itself against this disease in the future.

Changing viruses

Some viruses can't be kept out so easily. They keep changing their form. The antibody produced against the original form won't recognize the new form. Thus your body needs extra time to develop a new antibody for each form. The viruses that cause the common cold and influenza keep changing like this, so we have these illnesses again and again. The virus that causes AIDS can also change its form.

Special protection from disease

Doctors have a way of helping our bodies to fight against some diseases. This is done by giving people **vaccinations**. When you have a vaccination against cholera, a tiny amount of the cholera virus, which has been specially treated, is injected into your body through a needle. Your body then makes antibodies to fight the virus. So if the cholera virus tries to attack your body, you are immune to the disease that it causes.

Vaccinations are a major part of the worldwide fight against diseases, such as cholera, tuberculosis, and polio. Smallpox, the first disease for which a vaccine was used, has almost completely disappeared. But for some diseases, such as AIDS and the common cold, doctors still haven't found a vaccine.

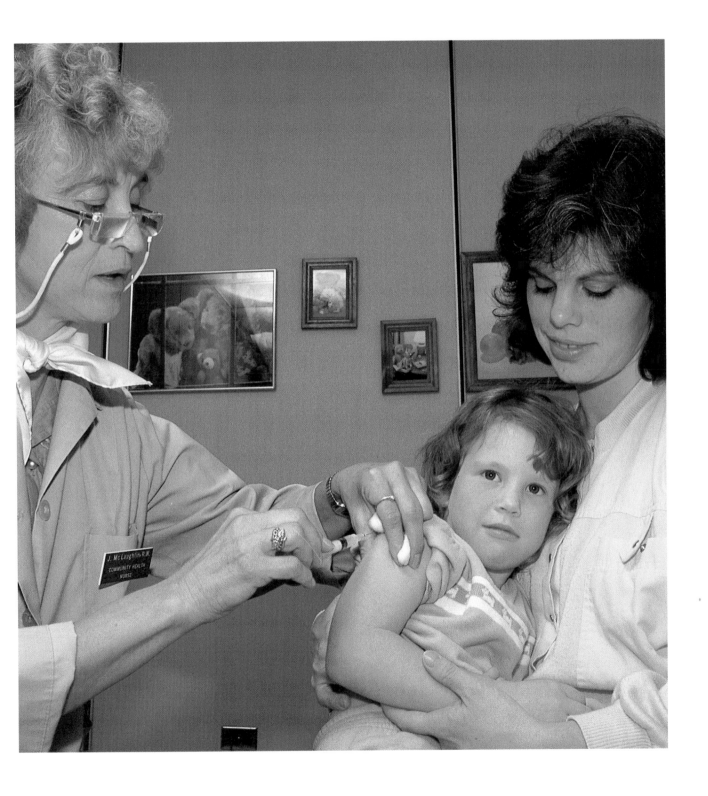

54

Find out more by looking at pages **48–49**

The larger invaders

You have seen how some diseases are caused by tiny microbes. Other diseases are caused by larger creatures called **protists** and also by worms. These larger invaders are sometimes more difficult to kill than the smaller ones.

Diseases caused by protists

Malaria and sleeping sickness are two diseases caused by protists. Protists are soft, jellylike creatures that usually need to be surrounded by plenty of water in order to survive. As our bodies contain lots of water, they can live inside us. Not all protists live inside people or other animals. Some live harmlessly in soil and water.

Protists are not as easily spread from one person to another as some microbes, such as bacteria and viruses. But they have special ways of infecting people. Some harmful protists are spread by biting insects. Tsetse flies spread sleeping sickness, and mosquitoes spread malaria and yellow fever.

When a mosquito bites a person, it sucks up blood. At the same time, it may infect the person's blood with the protist that causes yellow fever.

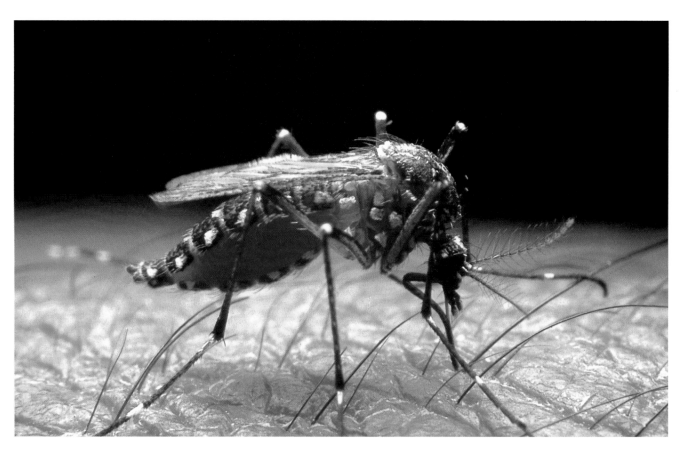

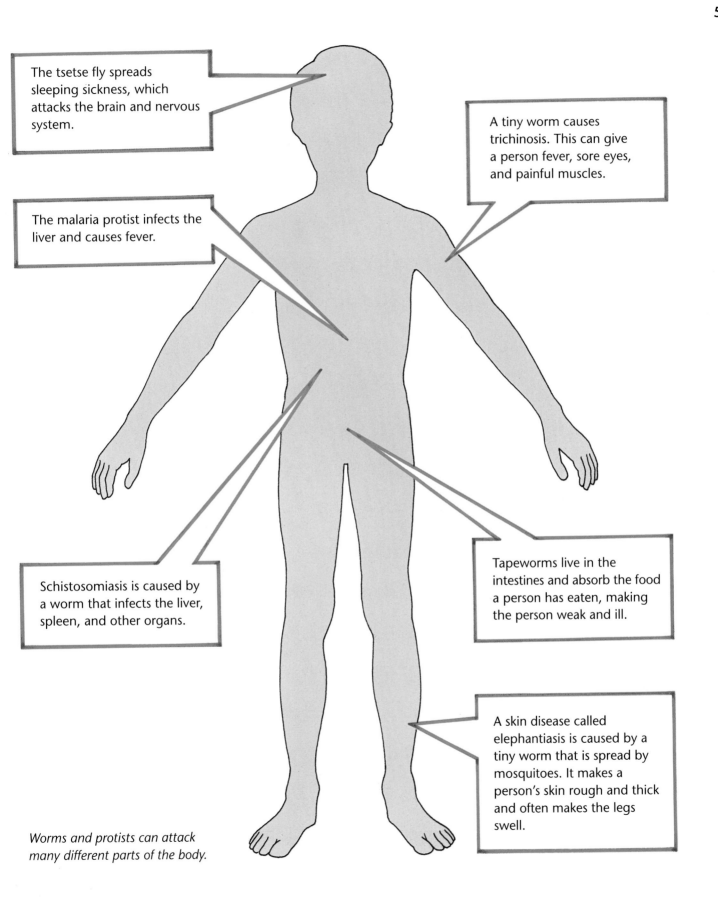

The tsetse fly spreads sleeping sickness, which attacks the brain and nervous system.

A tiny worm causes trichinosis. This can give a person fever, sore eyes, and painful muscles.

The malaria protist infects the liver and causes fever.

Schistosomiasis is caused by a worm that infects the liver, spleen, and other organs.

Tapeworms live in the intestines and absorb the food a person has eaten, making the person weak and ill.

A skin disease called elephantiasis is caused by a tiny worm that is spread by mosquitoes. It makes a person's skin rough and thick and often makes the legs swell.

Worms and protists can attack many different parts of the body.

Stop disease from spreading!

In most countries, there are government and private agencies that are concerned with the public health. They help prevent disease by purifying local water supplies, overseeing garbage disposal, keeping sewers in working order, and trying to control environmental pollution. Doctors and hospitals provide many services that help in disease prevention, too.

But there are many ways in which you can also help to prevent disease. Here are some important things to remember that will help protect you and your family from disease.

Washing your hands

Many microbes are spread by feces. However careful you are, you get some microbes on your hands when you go to the toilet. Always wash your hands with soap and water afterward.

Flies

Houseflies spread diseases when they land on food. Keep food covered up if there are flies around.

Pets

Pets can spread some diseases. Do not let a pet eat from your plate or lick your face around the mouth. Be careful about animal feces, too. If your pet uses part of your yard as a toilet, do not handle the soil there without gloves.

Water

Don't drink water from streams and rivers. Never drink pond or lake water. Before you swim anywhere, make sure that the water is free from harmful substances. If there is doubt, don't go swimming.

Coughs and sneezes

If you sneeze when you have a cold, you are showering everyone around you with thousands of microbes. Cover your mouth when you cough, and sneeze into a handkerchief.

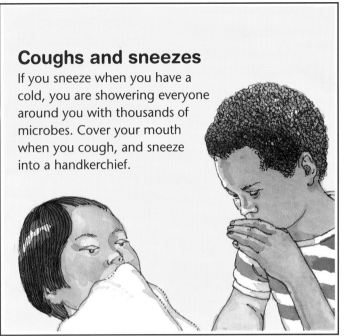

Keeping it to yourself

If you have a disease that can spread, try not to pass it on to anyone else! Stay away from other people as much as you can, until you are better.

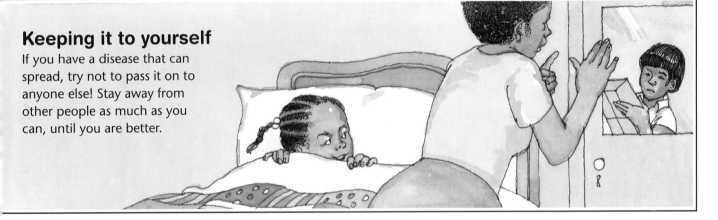

Cuts and scratches

Be careful with cuts and scratches because they are open to microbes. Cover them up with a bandage, especially if you are touching soil or swimming in a river. Cover up cuts if you are preparing food, because microbes can spread to the food.

Food

Always wash your hands before touching food. Always cook meat thoroughly. Do not keep cooked food for too long before eating it. Never store raw meat so that it can touch, or drip onto, cooked meat. It's a good idea to wash fruit and vegetables with clean water before you store them in the refrigerator or eat them. If you have a vegetable garden, don't let pets use it as a toilet.

The machine breaks down

Not all diseases are caused by things that invade our bodies. Some diseases occur because parts of our bodies simply stop working properly. Other diseases are caused by poisons in our food and drink, by lack of food, or even by the air we breathe. A disease may have many different causes. Sometimes the cause is unknown.

Diseases from birth

Some people are born with an illness that stays with them for their whole life. Other members of their family often suffer from the same problem. Many of these diseases can't be cured, but they can often be overcome in other ways. Some people have to stay on a special diet because they can't eat the foods that most people eat. Others have to take special medicines to keep their disease under control.

Allergies

Some people become ill when they come into contact with certain substances that are usually harmless. These substances include dust and pollen from plants. Some people's bodies react to these things as though they were harmful microbes. This causes a kind of illness called an **allergy.** Common allergies include hay fever, asthma, and some types of eczema.

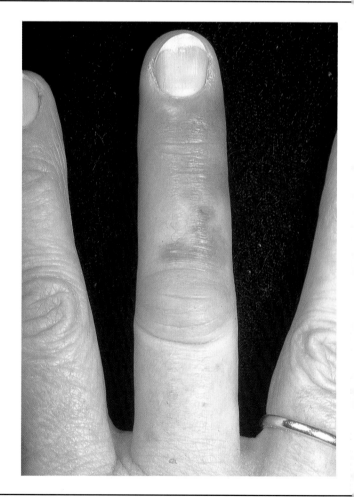

This finger has been stung by a bee. Allergy to the sting has made the finger red and swollen.

Cancer

Cancer is caused by cells that grow and divide without control. As uncontrolled divisions occur, a mass of cells is formed, called a **malignant tumor.** Doctors have discovered that certain chemicals in the world around us can make the growth of these tumors more likely. These chemicals are called **carcinogens.** Some people think that many of the chemicals that are added to food are carcinogens. This is why many people are careful to eat fruits and vegetables grown in fields where chemical fertilizers and pesticides have not been used.

Cure from the rain forests

The rain forests provide scientists with an enormous variety of plants. Some of these plants contain chemicals that can be used as medicines. Scientists are using some rain forest plants to fight cancer.

About 30 years ago, scientists who were trying to find a cure for cancer investigated a plant called the **rosy periwinkle.** This grows in the tropical forests of Madagascar, an island off the coast of Africa.

For many years, local healers had used this plant as a medicine. The scientists found that chemicals in the rosy periwinkle help to treat cancer. It is especially useful for treating children with cancer of the blood, known as leukemia, and for another type of cancer called Hodgkin's disease.

Another important anticancer drug comes from the bark of the Pacific yew, a small tree that grows in the Pacific Northwest region of the U.S. It is used to treat women with advanced breast and ovarian cancer.

Treatment using the rosy periwinkle and the Pacific yew has meant that doctors can help people fight cancer and live longer.

Chemicals in the rosy periwinkle help to treat leukemia.

People can buy many kinds of foods at this market in Kathmandu, in Nepal. You should eat a wide variety of food to keep your body healthy. Different foods provide different things your body needs.

Taking care of your body

You've seen that your body is like a wonderful machine, and you've found out how it works. Each part of your body has a special job to do. But in order for each part to work properly and in harmony with all the other parts, you must take care of your body.

To stay healthy, you need to eat meals that contain a balanced choice of foods. You need to get some kind of exercise regularly. And you must also rest, to allow your body to regain energy. It is important that you wash and keep yourself clean, to reduce the chances of catching a disease or an infection.

Eating the right foods

Many people are lucky enough to be able to eat all the right foods they need to keep alive and healthy. While you are growing, you need plenty of protein. This is found in foods such as fish, meat, milk, eggs, beans, and nuts. You should also eat at least five servings of fresh fruit and vegetables every day. You should eat regular meals and not go for long periods of time without eating.

Getting regular exercise

As well as eating the right foods, you must keep your muscles and joints healthy by getting lots of exercise. Regular exercise keeps your body strong and fit. It keeps the blood vessels healthy and makes the blood reach every part of your body. It helps you avoid putting on extra weight. Good activities include cycling, running, walking, and swimming.

Keeping clean

Make sure you keep yourself and your surroundings clean. This will help prevent bacteria, viruses, protists, and larger invaders from spreading through the environment and infecting you and others. Daily washing keeps your body free from dirt and prevents skin infections. The areas of your house where you eat and wash should always be kept clean.

Preventing illness

You can also be protected against some illnesses by being vaccinated. You can have vaccinations that will make you immune to certain viruses, such as measles, tuberculosis, and polio. There are laws that require vaccinations. If schools don't offer a vaccination program, then parents arrange for their children's vaccinations on their own.

Make sure you clean your teeth every day. Don't eat too many sugary foods, because they harm your teeth. It's a good idea to visit a dentist and have your teeth checked regularly.

Sleeping

Everyone needs sleep. Although the norm is eight hours a day, some people may need more, and others may require less. Sleep helps your body to recuperate, particularly the brain and the nervous system. Without sleep, you have less energy and feel tired. After hard work or exercise, you need to rest and relax. Relaxation can be just as important as sleep in helping you keep healthy.

A playground like this is an exciting place to run around and climb. You don't need a special place to play in but make sure that where you play is safe.

CONSERVATION

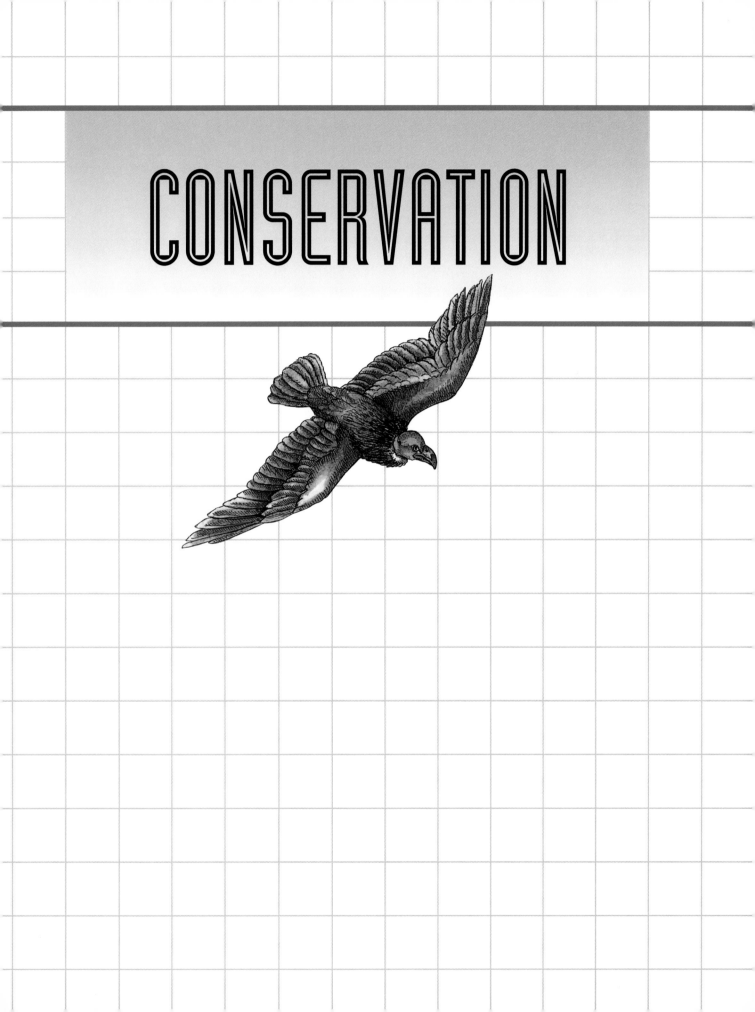

64

We gather crops such as corn, wheat, and rice to feed ourselves.

We dig and drill for coal, oil, and other minerals from below Earth's surface.

Life on Earth

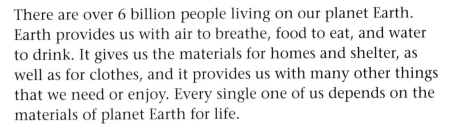

Earth provides food and shelter for over 6 billion people.

There are over 6 billion people living on our planet Earth. Earth provides us with air to breathe, food to eat, and water to drink. It gives us the materials for homes and shelter, as well as for clothes, and it provides us with many other things that we need or enjoy. Every single one of us depends on the materials of planet Earth for life.

One of the things everyone on Earth needs is space. We need space for a home, space in which to move around, and space in which to work. We need space for farms, where we can grow food, and space for factories. We need long stretches of space to build roads and wide areas of open space for parks. People have found many ways of using the space on our planet.

We also need to eat, to build homes, and to stay warm. To do these things, we use the land. We farm crops and herds of animals for food. We cut down trees and other plants. We dig up coal and drill for oil. We use up the things that Earth provides. We call these things Earth's **natural resources.**

Our future

Earth is important not just to the people who are living now, whom we call Earth's **population.** When you grow up, you may have children, and your children will probably have children. They, too, will need the things Earth provides. The world's population today is over 6 billion and is rising by about 1.4 percent each year. If this rate of growth continues, the population will reach about 10 billion by the year 2030. Will there still be food for everyone? Will Earth be a healthy and pleasant place to live? Will there be enough clean water, and will the air be safe enough to breathe?

Many animals share our planet with us. They provide us with meat, milk, and skins.

Find out more by looking at pages **68–69**

With the help of modern hospitals and medicines, many babies who might once have died of disease can now be kept alive and will grow to be healthy children.

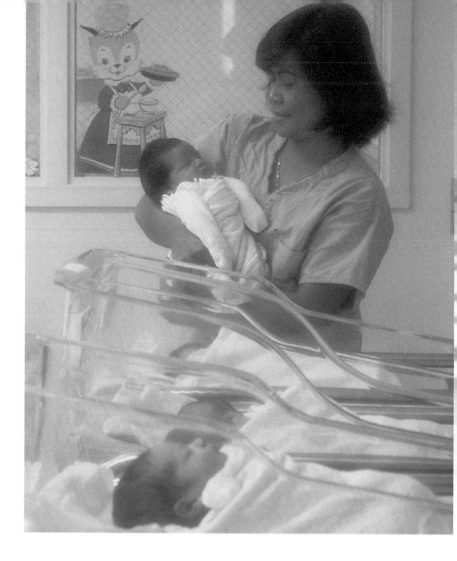

A crowded planet

For every single person alive in 1850, there are now about five people. Today the world's population is growing by 1.4 percent every year. Why is this happening?

A longer life

The main reason for the population increase is that people live longer. In the early 1900's, people who lived in the United States, for example, might expect to reach their 47th birthday. Since then, **life expectancy** has increased. People eat better food. They live and work in cleaner, healthier places. And they are helped by more medicines when they become ill. Today, U.S. citizens can look forward to their 76th birthday. Their life expectancy has increased by 29 years since the early 1900's! Many babies who might once have died of disease can now be kept alive and will grow to be healthy children.

Spreading homes

When too many people live in one place, life can become very difficult and unpleasant. In some places, there are so many people that there is not enough food or housing for everyone. Many families move to the cities, hoping to find work and homes. In time, the cities become overcrowded as more and more people arrive. More homes need to be built. Some people build their own homes using whatever materials they can find. The city spreads over more and more land. Good farming land is taken over to build houses, factories, and roads. As the world's population grows, there is less and less land available for farming.

The growth of towns and cities is called urban spread. It takes up land that could be used for food crops, and also destroys the places where plants and animals live.

Spoiling the land

For thousands of years, people hunted, fished, and farmed the land for food. They used plants to make cloth, paper, dyes, and medicines. They made tools and weapons from stone and metals. In time, they invented machines that were driven by water. Later, people learned how to power them with fuels like coal, gas, or oil. They built larger and larger cities and could reach them by road, rail, or air. They put up factories where hundreds of thousands of products could be made, like new types of clothing, furniture, and machines. And they built power stations to provide factories and homes with electricity.

Using up resources

For a long time, no one realized that all these activities were harming Earth. It was difficult to see just how quickly we were using up important natural resources like oil, coal, gas, and useful minerals. Everyone seemed to think there would always be new supplies, and few people worried about whether the resources could be saved or replaced.

Few people, too, worried about the spreading cities or about spoiling our surroundings. They did not take into account that plants and animals were disappearing as the population spread over the land. They did not realize the serious damage that they could cause the planet. They did not think about helping to save Earth and its resources, the work we now call **conservation.**

This aerial photograph of a lava quarry in Germany shows how digging for resources can destroy farmland.

Depending on each other

Do you live in the country? If so, you probably have a patch of land or a garden near your home where vegetables and other foods can be grown. But many people live in towns and cities without gardens. They depend on farmers in the countryside to grow enough food for everyone.

Protecting our crops

Farmers try to grow the best crops on their farmland. But they need to protect their crops from pests and diseases. Some farmers spray their crops with special liquids called **pesticides**. Many of these sprays are poisonous. They will kill the pests and diseases, but, unfortunately, they have other effects.

1. The mice have found a home in this field of grass, though they have to beware of owls.

2. The mice are pests because they eat the farmer's crops. The farmer has sprayed his crops with pesticide.

3. The mice eat the grain, but it does not kill them immediately.

Natural habitat

The farmer's field was a home, or **habitat**, to many living things, both plants and animals, that depended on each other in many ways. It was a place where mice, for example, found food and shelter. When the farmer plowed the land, he destroyed the wild plants that grew in the field. Animals such as the mice that fed on these plants had to go elsewhere to find food. Other animals, like owls who fed on the mice, had to move away also. What the farmer did affected not just one kind of plant or animal, but all the plants and animals living in the habitat.

Breaking the food chain

Eventually the farmer's field may once again attract mice. They will feed on grain and use the tall cereal grasses to build their nests. Then owls might return to feed on the mice. The farm cat might also eat the mice.

Plants and animals that provide food for each other are members of a food chain. If the food chain is broken, every animal in it will suffer. What do you think happens when the farmer poisons the mice?

4. A mouse that is weakened by the poison is easy prey for an owl. The owl that eats a poisoned mouse eventually dies from the poison.

5. The farmer's cat eats another poisoned mouse and dies. The farmer is pleased to be rid of the mice. But he has killed two animals that would have helped him. Owls and cats help to keep down farm pests.

Find out more by looking
at pages **68–69**
74–75

Some scientists are worried that the numbers of koalas may increase enormously. If this happens, the koalas' food supply, the eucalyptus tree, may run out, and koalas would starve.

Disappearing life

Can you imagine being the last person alive on Earth? You would be the last member of your animal group, or **species**, called *Homo sapiens*. Many animals and plants once found on Earth are already extinct. Over time, new species developed in their place. But today, thousands of animal species and even more plants are in danger of dying out, and there is little hope that they will be replaced.

Why do animals become extinct?

The dinosaurs became extinct about 65 million years ago. Perhaps a natural disaster or a change in climate destroyed their habitat, or their food supply disappeared. Many animals face these threats today. Lion tamarins in Brazil are losing their habitat because people are cutting down the forest for timber and farmland. In China, giant pandas live on a few species of bamboo. Some kinds of bamboo flower once every 100 years and then die. It may be years before the seeds grow again. Flowering occurred in the late 1970's, and hundreds of giant pandas starved. By the early 1990's, fewer than 1,000 giant pandas remained in the wild.

Endangered plant life

Some species of plant life have become extinct because of natural causes, but the activities of human beings have endangered many more. For example, humans have cut down forests, drained wetlands, built houses, and created much pollution. As a result, some plant species have declined greatly in numbers, and others are extinct. Plants facing extinction include the black cabbage tree, the St. Helena redwood, and several California manzanitas.

In the late 1970's, large areas of bamboo in China flowered and died. Many giant pandas starved before new shoots could grow again.

The lion tamarin lives in the rain forests of eastern Brazil. It is becoming very rare, as people destroy more and more of its forest habitat.

Tropical rain forests are disappearing fast. People are cutting down the trees to make farmland and to build cities.

Animals in danger

Animal species that are in danger of dying out are called **endangered species.** People are one of the greatest threats to the survival of some animals. Many animals are endangered because of our activities. We destroy their habitats, disturb their food chains, and even hunt some of them.

Disturbing wildlife

In the past, tigers, lions, and leopards were killed for their skins or for sport. Many kinds of animals are still killed by human hunters. Illegal hunters, called **poachers,** still shoot elephants and rhinoceroses for their tusks and horns.

Hunting is just one way in which we disturb wildlife. Farming the land, using poisons, cutting down trees, collecting rare species—all these activities can threaten the existence of much of the world's wildlife.

Protecting wildlife habitats

Nothing can be done about the plant and animal species that are already extinct. But we can protect those that are endangered. The governments of many countries have already passed laws against hunting endangered animals.

Project Tiger

In the early 1900's, there were many thousands of tigers in Asia. But thousands were hunted and killed. Then people cleared the forests where they lived and more died. By 1988, there were fewer than 5,000 left. Many people were concerned that tigers were becoming extinct.

The government of India is trying to save the country's tiger population with a plan called Project Tiger. In 1973, large areas of land were set aside to create special tiger reserves. These are places where tigers could not be hunted.

The number of tigers has increased inside these reserves. But tigers are still endangered, and poachers continue to hunt them. Many conservationists fear that there will not be enough tigers left to reproduce and keep the species healthy. The tiger might still become extinct in the wild.

tiger

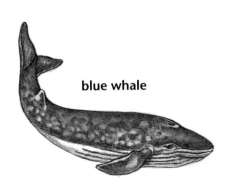

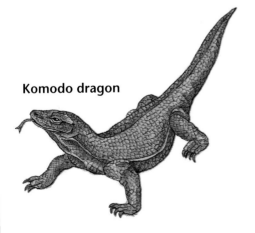

Endangered species—animals in danger

Animal	Habitat
California condor	Most California condors once lived only in captivity, but some are now being released into the wild.
Philippine eagle	This eagle is found in the forests of the Philippines.
Queen Alexandra's birdwing butterfly	Queen Alexandra's birdwing butterflies live in the forests of Papua New Guinea.
European lynx	This lynx was once common in Europe and northern Asia.
Mountain gorilla	Mountain gorillas inhabit the forests of east-central Africa.
Rhinoceros	Three species of rhinoceros live in Asia, and two species live in Africa.
Blue whale	The oceans of the world are the home of the blue whale.
Giant panda	Giant pandas are found only in bamboo forests in the mountains of western and southwestern China.
Orangutan	The orangutan lives deep in the forests of Borneo and Sumatra.
Polar bear	Polar bears live on the cold shores of the Arctic Ocean.
Marine otter	The marine otter lives in the waters off South America.
Komodo dragon	Komodo dragons live on the islands of Indonesia.

California condor

rhinoceros

blue whale

Komodo dragon

Find out more by looking at pages **78–79** **80–81**

Wildflowers are beginning to grow on this piece of land, which people had damaged. But it will be many years before the land recovers completely.

Protecting plants

Plants are some of the living things that are most important for our survival on Earth. Without plants, there would be no life on our planet. The food we eat comes from plants or from animals that eat plants. The oxygen we breathe has been formed by plants over billions of years. Even some of our building materials (such as wood) and clothing (such as cotton) come from plants.

How can we help the plant kingdom? We can stop gathering wild flowers to decorate our homes. Flowers produce the seeds that will grow into new plants, so they should be left to bloom and shed their seeds where they grow. We should try not to harm birds. They eat the fruits that contain seeds and scatter the seeds in their droppings. When we walk through the countryside, we should follow well-worn paths. Then we will not disturb the wildlife. We should never start fires. Fires can spread quickly, destroying everything in their path.

Protect nature

Here are six, easy-to-remember rules that will help you protect the plants and animals in the places you may visit.

Never eat wild berries, fruits, or fungi without asking an adult first. Some are poisonous!

1. Do not pick flowers.

2. Do not take birds' eggs.

3. Keep to well-worn paths.

4. Never start fires.

5. Do not eat anything strange.

6. Take your litter home.

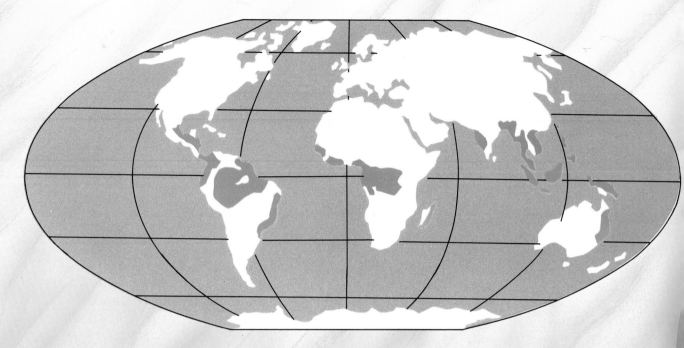

There are thick tropical rain forests near the equator in Central and South America, Africa, Asia, and on Pacific Islands. About half of the world's species of plants and animals live in the tropical rain forests.

Tropical rain forests

Vast regions of Earth have plenty of sunshine and rain. This hot, wet climate makes trees and plants grow quickly, forming huge, dense forests. These are known as **tropical rain forests.** Mahogany and rosewood are kinds of trees known as hardwoods. These trees grow well in the tropics. They provide a good habitat for animals. Many animals, such as parrots, monkeys, eagles, and bats, find food and shelter high up in the trees.

These trees also provide us with a valuable harvest of good-quality timber. For this reason, vast stretches of forests are being cut down. Other areas are cleared to provide land for farming or for mining rich ores. More forest is cleared to make way for roads.

Meanwhile, what is happening to the plant and animal life of the forest? Many of the plants have been lost forever. Those animals that depend on the plants for food must move to remaining parts of the forest. They will be followed by other animals in the food chain. Soon the remaining forest is crowded and unable to support all the animals that are trying to live in it.

Find out more by looking at pages **72 – 73**
80 – 81

No protection

Much of the land that has been cleared is used for farming. But without the protection of the trees, the soil quickly dries out and breaks up in the heat and wind. After a few years, the soil is worn out, and the farmer must clear new land.

Millons of acres of tropical rain forests are destroyed each year. This is a serious problem because trees take in carbon dioxide, so if there are fewer trees, there will be more carbon dioxide in the air. Carbon dioxide traps heat from the sun, so the world's climate will become hotter in the future. The destruction of the rain forests is one of the world's most serious conservation problems.

Machines like these claw their way through the rain forests. They destroy about 50 million acres (20 million hectares) of rain forest each year.

Saving the forests

What can we do to help save the tropical rain forests? There are two ways to prevent them from disappearing altogether. One way is to make sure that no more trees are cut down. The other is to replant trees on forestland that has been cleared.

If we look after the forests, they can still provide us with timber. The older trees can be felled, leaving the younger trees with room to grow. This way, the forests will provide a continuous home for plant and animal life. The growing trees will use up carbon dioxide and give out oxygen. Trees can also be planted to replace those that have been cut down.

National parks

In Brazil, people are experimenting with different types of trees to help replant the forest quickly.

The governments of countries in South America, central Africa, and Southeast Asia have started to protect their rain forests. They have turned areas of forest into national parks, where all tree-felling and other activities that could damage the forest and its wildlife are strictly controlled.

Students in Vietnam are replanting an area of forest destroyed during the Vietnam War.

Putting trees back

In Vietnam, in Southeast Asia, large areas of rain forest have already been destroyed by clearance and also by war. But the Vietnamese people are beginning to replant the forests. They have planted fast-growing trees in the cleared areas. These kinds of trees are not usually found in rain forests. They do not support the same animals or plants. But as these trees grow, they provide protection for other, slower-growing plants. After many, many years, there could be new rain forests.

Putting animals back

The animal life of the rain forest is more difficult to bring back. Before they were destroyed, the forests in Vietnam provided a safe habitat for thousands of species, from tigers, primates, and elephants to tiny insects. If replanting the forests succeeds, it will be necessary to bring animals from other rain forests—or zoos—to restock them.

The government of Vietnam has also set aside large areas of land to protect native plant and animal species. They have also made laws and regulations that protect many of the forest primates from being hunted and traded illegally.

Frozen habitats

The region at the North Pole and the region around the South Pole are two of the coldest places on Earth. In winter, the Arctic is an ocean of ice that stretches to the northern coasts of North America and Russia. Antarctica is a huge continent that is always covered by a layer of ice.

You may not think that much plant or animal life could survive in such icy conditions. But the Arctic and Antarctica are important wildlife habitats. There are some animals living in these places that are not found anywhere else on Earth.

The Arctic

Ever since oil was discovered under the Arctic Ocean, the pattern of Arctic wildlife has been changed forever. Plants have been destroyed as land is cleared for building. Animals have been frightened away from their breeding grounds.

Arctic skua

Arctic fox

caribou

polar bear

snowy owl

ptarmigan

walrus

ringed seal

Arctic hare

bowhead whale

saxifrage

Arctic poppy

blue whale

albatross

killer whale

elephant seal

Antarctica

Since 1959, Antarctica has been protected by the Antarctic Treaty. The 12 countries that had been working in Antarctica pledged to pursue only peaceful activities, such as scientific study and exploration. The treaty includes laws to protect Antarctic plants and animals. In 1998, an international agreement setting aside Antarctica as a global wilderness preserve went into effect. Part of the Antarctic Treaty, it forbids mining and oil drilling, pesticides, and other threats to wildlife.

Ross seal

leopard seal

Adélie penguins

Weddell seal

snow petrel

emperor penguins

84

Find out more by looking at pages **86–87**

The ozone layer

During the late 1970's, scientists began to notice something strange happening in Earth's atmosphere. They were surprised to see a "hole" appearing each spring in a layer of gas that surrounds Earth. This layer of gas is called the **ozone layer.**

The scientists noticed that the ozone layer appeared to be getting thinner and thinner. The problem was most serious over Antarctica. Here they found the ozone layer was thinner each spring. There are fears that the ozone layer may eventually thin out over more populated areas. Though these "holes" may be smaller than the one over Antarctica, there is enough cause for concern.

Dangerous holes

The ozone layer lies in the stratosphere, between 9 and 18 miles (15 and 30 kilometers) above Earth's surface. This layer shields us from some of the **ultraviolet rays** from the sun. These rays can cause lighter-skinned people to get darker and even burn in the sunlight. Too many ultraviolet rays are bad for everyone. In addition to sunburn, they can cause some kinds of skin cancers.

During the late 1970's, scientists observed that the ozone layer over Antarctica had become thinner. Since then, it has become thinner still, allowing harmful ultraviolet rays from the sun to pass through the atmosphere.

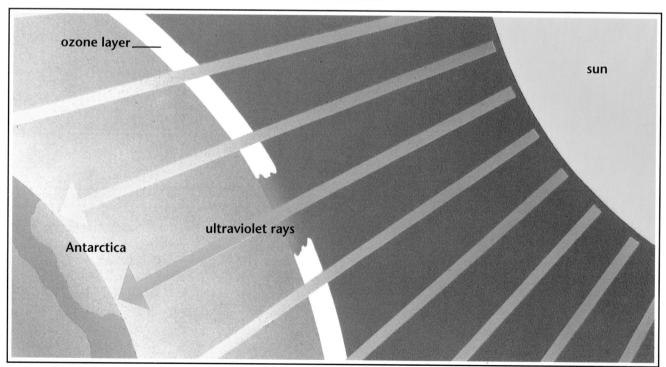

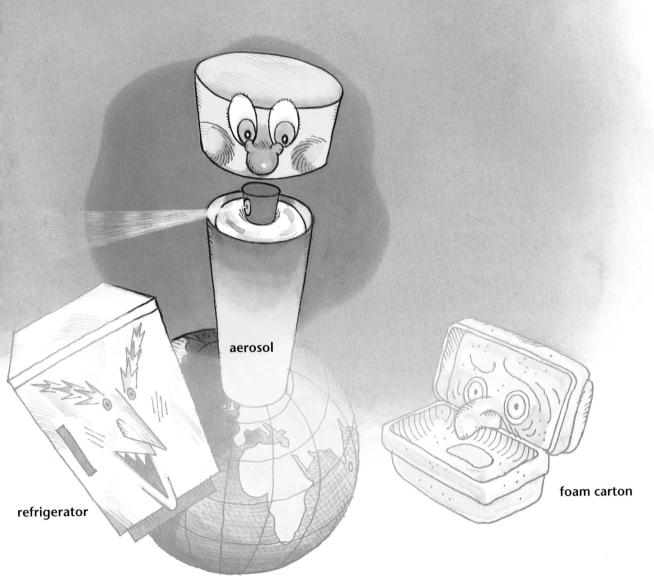

aerosol

refrigerator

foam carton

Chlorofluorocarbons (CFC's) from aerosol sprays, refrigerators, and foam cartons destroy ozone.

Harmful chemicals

No one knows for sure what is causing the ozone layer to become thinner. But we do know that certain chemicals make ozone break down and disappear. These harmful chemicals, called **chlorofluorocarbons** (CFC's), have been used in aerosol sprays, air conditioning units and refrigerators, and to make plastic cartons and other products.

Some countries, including the United States, banned CFC sprays many years ago. Other countries have slowly followed their example. By 1996, most industrialized countries ended the production of CFC's. However, CFC's already in use continue to damage the ozone layer. For instance, numerous refrigerators now in use have CFC's safely contained. But when a refrigerator is thrown away or broken up, the CFC's are released into the atmosphere.

Living in a greenhouse

The world is getting warmer. If you enjoy warm weather, you may think this is good news—but it's not. Some experts say that over the last hundred years, temperatures on Earth have increased by 2.7 to 10 degrees Fahrenheit (1.5 to 5.6 degrees Celsius). Earth's atmosphere is warming up, just as if it was trapped inside a greenhouse. This warming process is often called the **greenhouse effect.**

Why is Earth warming up?

More of the sun's energy is reaching Earth's atmosphere because the ozone layer is becoming thinner. But there is another reason why Earth is warming up. When we burn fuels like coal, oil, gas, or wood, carbon dioxide is released into the atmosphere. Plants use carbon dioxide to help make their food. So tropical rain forests take in large amounts of carbon dioxide from the atmosphere, but at the same time people are cutting down vast areas of these forests. Why is this harmful?

The greenhouse effect

Earth is warmed by the sun. Most of the heat is sent back, or **radiated**, into the atmosphere. Carbon dioxide in the atmosphere traps some of this heat, preventing it from escaping into space. This keeps Earth warm. But if there is too much carbon dioxide in the atmosphere, it will trap too much heat, and Earth's atmosphere will become too hot.

What could happen?

If Earth's atmosphere becomes much warmer, the ice in the Arctic and in Antarctica will begin to melt. This will raise the level of the seas all over the world. A rise of only a few inches could flood many coastlines. Low-lying coastal towns and cities would be endangered by floods, and so would large areas of farmland. If the seas became warmer, the sea animals and plants would be affected. And many might not be able to survive at all. In other parts of the world, a lack of rain might mean that farmland will become too dry and dusty.

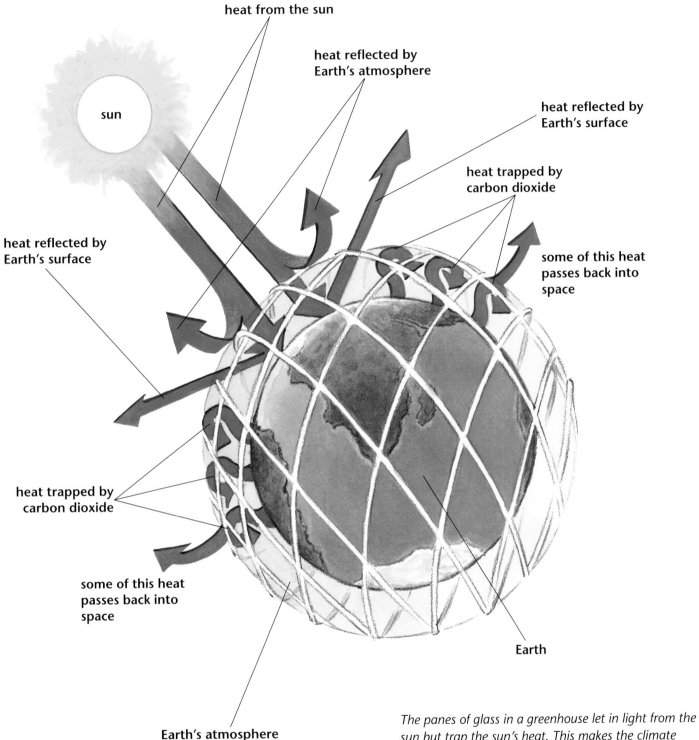

heat from the sun

heat reflected by
Earth's atmosphere

heat reflected by
Earth's surface

heat trapped by
carbon dioxide

sun

heat reflected by
Earth's surface

some of this heat
passes back into
space

heat trapped by
carbon dioxide

some of this heat
passes back into
space

Earth

Earth's atmosphere

The panes of glass in a greenhouse let in light from the sun but trap the sun's heat. This makes the climate inside the greenhouse hot. In a similar way, Earth's atmosphere lets in sunlight but carbon dioxide traps some of this heat and sends it back to Earth's surface. This is the "greenhouse effect." If there is too much carbon dioxide in the atmosphere, it will trap too much heat, and Earth's atmosphere will become too hot. This is called global warming.

Farming the land

Day by day, there are more and more people to be fed. Farming produces most of the food that is needed. In many parts of the world, such as the open grasslands of the United States, Russia, Canada, and Australia, huge areas are plowed and planted with crops, year after year. This kind of farming is called **intensive agriculture.**

Intensive agriculture produces huge harvests for only a few years. Farmers grow the same crop every year. The crops need substances called **nutrients** found in the soil to grow. In time, the growing plants use up the soil's nutrients. Fertilizers are added, but the soil still becomes worn out. Trees and hedges that divided the fields thin out and die. The soil is then swept away more easily by strong winds and rain.

Spreading disease

Some pests feed on one particular crop. If the same crop is planted each year, the pests will thrive. They often carry diseases to the new crop. If different crops are planted each year, the pests are not able to feed, and the diseases begin to die out.

Crops, such as corn, can be ruined by disease.

Intensive farming produces huge harvests for a few years. Combine harvesters gather tons of grain from enormous fields.

When too many cattle graze on the land, the grass cannot grow and the soil is easily swept away by the wind and rain.

Damaging the land

Some areas of grassland are not used for growing crops. Often farmers raise sheep or cattle here instead. These animals will provide us with food, but first we must feed them. Some cattle are fed with corn and specially prepared feeds. Some cattle graze the land. Cattle that are kept for beef can eat more than 37 pounds (17 kilograms) of feed each day.

There are 1.25 billion cattle in the world. Imagine how much grass they are eating. This can be a problem in the drier areas of Asia and South America where large herds are kept. Here, intensive cattle farming is damaging the land. The grass animals graze on needs to be left alone for a while so that it can grow again. If the animals are not moved to new pastures, no grass is left to trap moisture and hold the soil together. The land becomes dry and **overgrazed.** Then the soil can be swept away by the wind and the rain.

The farmer has sprayed fertilizer onto his field. Rain falls and washes the fertilizer down into the soil.

Feeding the land

After several years, intensive agriculture can leave the soil exhausted. Before the farmer can sow a field with a new crop, the nutrients that have been taken out with the last harvest must be put back. **Chemical fertilizers** may be added to the soil to help the crops grow well.

Weeds and pests

Unwanted weeds growing in the field also take nutrients from the soil. The farmer may use a **chemical weedkiller** on a field to get rid of the weeds. **Chemical pesticides** protect the crops from pests and diseases. However, some pests and diseases come to resist the chemical sprays. So, in time, the farmer needs to spray the crops with stronger pesticides.

These chemicals are taken in by plants and so find their way into the food we eat. Some chemicals are washed through the soil into streams and rivers, where they can poison the wildlife. Sometimes, chemicals reach our reservoirs and are pumped to our homes in the water supply.

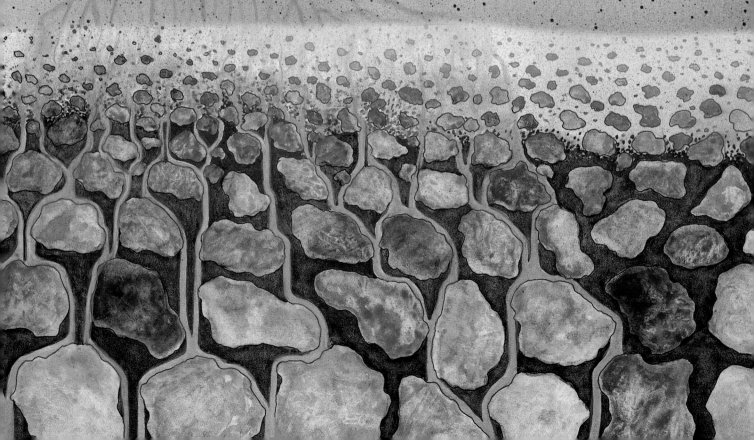

Farming without chemicals

Most farmers today use chemical fertilizers to boost crop production. But others worry about the bad effects of these chemicals on people and the environment. They are concerned that using chemicals over a long period of time makes the soil unhealthy by robbing it of the nutrients plants need to grow.

To avoid using chemicals, some farmers are turning to **organic fertilizers.** Organic fertilizer contains decomposed plant and animal material. It also contains ground minerals. Organic fertilizer helps plants grow strong and healthy. It also helps keep the soil healthy, too, by supplying it with nutrients so that it will not become exhausted.

Some farmers use organic fertilizers because they are healthier for the environment than chemical fertilizers.

Looking after the land

The land that we need for growing food is very important. We can't afford to spoil it. There are many ways in which farmers are making better use of the land and growing good crops without the help of factory-made chemicals. If farmed carefully, the land will go on giving us enough food to eat for thousands of years.

You will need:

three small plant pots

three saucers

some soil

sand

powdered clay

nine beans

three labels

water

notebook and pencil

Testing your soil

Try this experiment to see how well the same kind of plant grows in different types of soil.

1. Fill the first pot with soil. Fill the second pot with a mixture of soil and powdered clay. In the third pot, put a mixture of soil and sand.

2. Use your pencil to make three small holes in the soil of each pot. Drop a bean into each hole and cover it lightly with soil. Label the pots and check them every day. Water the pots enough to keep the soil moist.

3. When the seedlings begin to grow, measure their height, count the number of leaves, and look at their color. Record your observations in your notebook.

Crop rotation

One method of careful farming is called **crop rotation.** Different kinds of plants take different nutrients from the soil and leave others behind. The same crop planted year after year takes out the same nutrients. But different crops, like corn and alfalfa, can be planted on the same piece of land. One year, corn is planted. This will take out certain nutrients from the soil. The following year, alfalfa will be planted. The alfalfa will put back the nutrients absorbed by the corn.

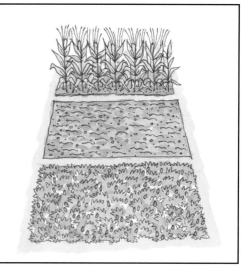

Alley cropping

Another farming method is to mix trees and crops on the same piece of land. In Africa, this is called **alley cropping.** Rows of quick-growing, deep-rooted trees are planted a few yards apart, with rows of crops such as sorghum in between. The trees help to prevent the soil from being blown or washed away. Their leaves rot and add to the **humus** in the soil. Humus is made from dead plant matter. Tree shoots provide animal food and fuel for cooking. The trees and the sorghum take different nutrients from the soil, so they can grow side by side.

Contour plowing

Sometimes, surface soil, or **topsoil,** is washed away by rain. This is called **water erosion.** Farmers can help prevent water erosion by plowing across a slope instead of up and down it. This is called **contour plowing.** When it rains, water does not run down the hill, washing away soil as it goes. Instead, it is caught in the furrows and soaks in, leaving the soil behind. Contour plowing also prevents streams from getting blocked by washed-away soil and flooding low-lying land.

When land is overfarmed or over-grazed, the topsoil turns to dust, which blows away in the wind. The layer of soil left behind is baked hard by the sun. In time, it cracks. Any rain that falls cannot soak in, and it flows away.

Spreading deserts

Until about 6,000 years ago, the Sahara in northern Africa was a fertile plain. Many animals roamed across the grassland. There were also many people, herding their animals from pasture to pasture or farming the land. Then the climate began to change. Less rain fell, and the dry land turned to desert.

Today, the Sahara is Earth's largest desert. And it is growing in size every year.

Why does the land turn to desert?

About one-fifth of Earth's land area is desert. Each year, these desert areas of the world are becoming larger. As the soil dries up, the edges of the desert spread and the land can no longer provide food for grazing animals. This is caused partly by changes in the world's climate. But it is made worse by people who have dug up the grassland for farming or allowed too many animals to graze on it.

The moving sands

One of the areas where the desert has spread recently is the Sahel, an area south of the Sahara, in Africa. It is an area of grassland which has often suffered from **drought**, long periods of no rain. Since 1968, the Sahel has suffered from especially bad drought, as well as other changes in the climate. The land has dried up and has begun to turn into desert. **Overgrazing** has created more bare soil.

New wells were dug, but the surrounding land was grazed bare as people gathered with their animals. New crops were introduced and fields were no longer left to rest. The few remaining trees were cut down to be used for fuel. Winds from the Sahara blew away the dry topsoil of the Sahel and left barren sand. In the end, there was not enough grassland left to support the people who lived there. Some moved away, but millions of people and animals have died since 1968.

How the Sahel became a desert

1. When the Sahel was grassland, it could support a small number of farmers. When the drought became worse, people settled near wells. They cut the trees for fuel. Their animals cleared the grass and trampled the soil.

2. As the population increased, more land was cleared. New crops were grown, which did not allow the soil to rest and regain its nutrients.

3. Winds from the Sahara brought sandstorms, which covered the dry, dusty Sahel soil with sand. People who could not move away with their animals slowly starved.

Find out more by looking at pages **98–99**

Fresh air?

How fresh is the air where you live? If you live in the countryside, it might be clean and fresh. All living things must have fresh air to live. Air contains oxygen, which people and animals need, and carbon dioxide, which plants use to make energy from sunlight. There are small amounts of other gases in clean air, too, but these are harmless to us.

However, in and near towns and cities, the air contains many other substances that can harm us. One of these is **sulfur dioxide**, which comes from burning some types of coal and oil. Sulfur dioxide is often an ingredient in another type of air pollution, called **smog.** Smog can build up over an area and cause illness and even death.

What causes most pollution? Although some natural substances, such as dust, pollen, and ash, pollute the air, people create by far most of the harmful pollutants. Power plants that burn coal and oil to produce energy churn out huge amounts of pollution. Factories, the burning of wastes, and the use of chemicals also add to the problem.

Sources of pollution

Many things people do create air pollution. Chemical sprays used to start fires on charcoal grills release pollutants into the air. In rural areas and in developing countries, burning forests and grasslands to clear areas for farming also causes air pollution. So does burning garbage.

Transportation fumes

One of the main causes of air pollution is exhaust fumes from cars, airplanes, ships, and trains. When gasoline or diesel oil burns, it produces a number of harmful chemicals, such as **nitrogen oxide** and a poisonous gas called **carbon monoxide.** Exhaust fumes also contain carbon dioxide and a group of chemicals called **hydrocarbons.** Some scientists believe hydrocarbons can cause cancer and other illnesses.

When the sun is shining, hydrocarbons can also react with nitrogen oxides. This chemical reaction produces a form of oxygen called **ozone.** Ozone is an ingredient of smog.

Reducing air pollution

Though air pollution is still a serious problem, many countries are working to reduce it. Many electric power plants, factories, and facilities that burn wastes are equipped with devices called **scrubbers.** Scrubbers remove sulfur dioxide and other pollutants before the wastes are released into the air.

Governments also have passed regulations to cut down on air pollution. For example, most American-made cars have been equipped with anti-pollution devices called **catalytic converters.** These devices reduce the amount of pollution from automobile engines.

There are other ways to reduce air pollution. The equipment we use to manufacture things, and to heat and cool buildings, all burns fuel. Engineers can design equipment that uses less fuel, which helps conserve our fuel supply and reduces the amount of pollutants released into the air. People can help, too, by driving their cars only when necessary, carpooling whenever they can, and using public transportation. Recycling also reuses some wastes that otherwise might have been burned.

In the United States, laws have been passed to improve the quality of the air. These laws set specific guidelines for air quality. They also require the sale of cleaner burning fuels, and encourage the reduction of polluting chemicals that power plants can release into the air.

Acid rain

Poisonous gases and other chemicals pour into the atmosphere every day. These are the waste products from our power stations, factories, and cars. Two of these waste gases, sulfur dioxide and nitrogen oxide, collect in the atmosphere. They then mix with the moisture in the air to become **sulfuric acid** and **nitric acid**. These acids are absorbed by rain clouds and fall to the ground again as **acid rain**.

Acid rain forms when water vapor in the air reacts with compounds such as sulfur dioxide and nitrogen oxide. These compounds come mostly from burning coal, gasoline, and oil. Most automobiles, factories, and power plants burn these fuels for energy.

Where does acid rain fall?

The areas where most acid rain falls are the eastern part of North America, central and northwestern Europe, and parts of Asia. Acid rain falling on North America comes from the industrial cities of the United States. Much of the acid rain in northwestern Europe has drifted from Germany.

Damaging the environment

Acid rain can cause serious damage. It kills trees and destroys many wildlife habitats. Forest areas in eastern North America, central Europe, and parts of Asia have been damaged by acid rain.

When acid rain falls into lakes and rivers, it harms fish, plants, and other freshwater life. In cities, acid rain can even eat away at stone buildings.

When acid rain falls into lakes and rivers, it harms fish, plants, and other freshwater life. In cities, acid rain can even eat away at stone buildings.

How can we prevent acid rain?

Scientists and engineers are discovering many new ways to reduce the air pollution that causes acid rain. One way is to wash the sulfur out of the smoke created from burning coal. This prevents the sulfur from entering the atmosphere.

Another way to prevent acid rain is to find new sources of energy besides fossil fuels. Hydroelectricity uses the power of water to make energy. Nuclear power creates energy by splitting atoms. Scientists are also experimenting with windmills and solar energy.

Because acid rain passes from one country to another, it is an international problem. To solve it completely, all countries must cooperate with one another. Many countries have already agreed to reduce the pollution that causes acid rain.

Waste gases from power stations and factory chimneys rise into the air. The gases mix with water vapor in the clouds.

The wind carries these clouds great distances. The rain that falls from them is a weak acid. This acid rain damages the countryside.

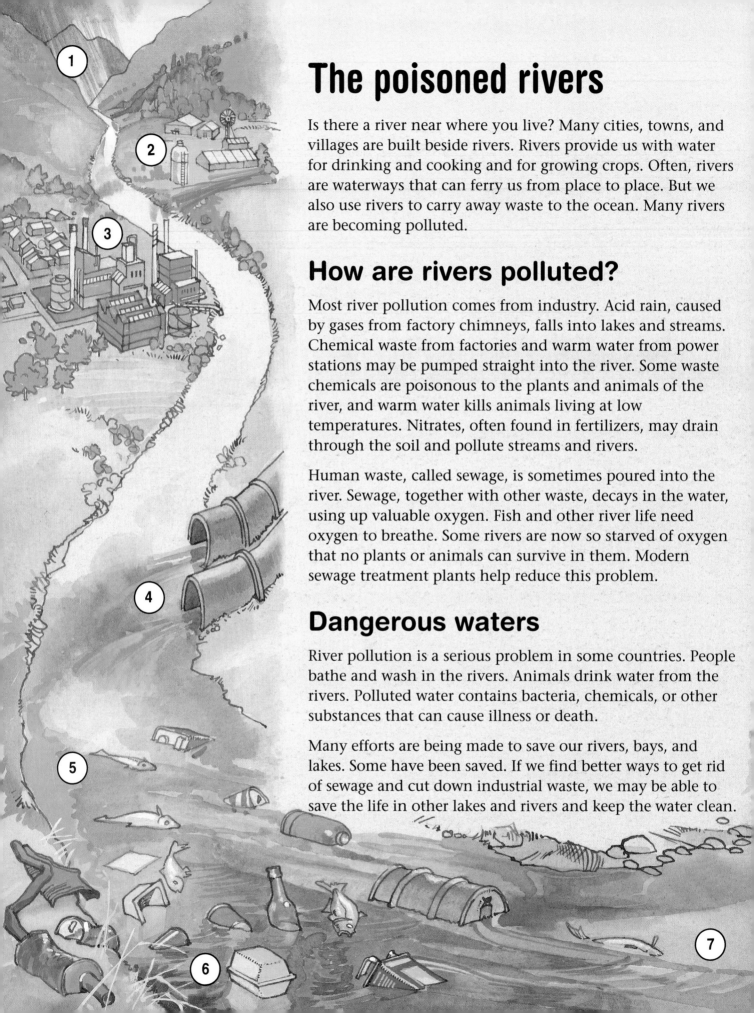

The poisoned rivers

Is there a river near where you live? Many cities, towns, and villages are built beside rivers. Rivers provide us with water for drinking and cooking and for growing crops. Often, rivers are waterways that can ferry us from place to place. But we also use rivers to carry away waste to the ocean. Many rivers are becoming polluted.

How are rivers polluted?

Most river pollution comes from industry. Acid rain, caused by gases from factory chimneys, falls into lakes and streams. Chemical waste from factories and warm water from power stations may be pumped straight into the river. Some waste chemicals are poisonous to the plants and animals of the river, and warm water kills animals living at low temperatures. Nitrates, often found in fertilizers, may drain through the soil and pollute streams and rivers.

Human waste, called sewage, is sometimes poured into the river. Sewage, together with other waste, decays in the water, using up valuable oxygen. Fish and other river life need oxygen to breathe. Some rivers are now so starved of oxygen that no plants or animals can survive in them. Modern sewage treatment plants help reduce this problem.

Dangerous waters

River pollution is a serious problem in some countries. People bathe and wash in the rivers. Animals drink water from the rivers. Polluted water contains bacteria, chemicals, or other substances that can cause illness or death.

Many efforts are being made to save our rivers, bays, and lakes. Some have been saved. If we find better ways to get rid of sewage and cut down industrial waste, we may be able to save the life in other lakes and rivers and keep the water clean.

The river's journey

This river is clean when it starts its journey to the ocean. Many plants and fish live in the water.

1. Rain clouds carry acid rain from the towns on the other side of the mountains. The acid rain falls in the streams that feed the river.

2. The river passes a farm where rain washes chemicals into it.

3. Farther on, the river passes a town where chemicals from factories pollute it.

4. Then sewage enters the river and decays. Foam comes from detergents that the waste-treatment system has been unable to break down.

5. By this time, all the fish have been poisoned. There are no plants on the riverbank either.

6. People see that the river is a dump and throw even more garbage into it.

7. By the time the water reaches the sea, it's in a terrible mess!

Waste from copper mines has turned the water of the Rio Tinto in Spain deep red. People have mined near this river for thousands of years. Its name means "colored river."

Find out more by looking at pages **100–101**

The dirty oceans

You probably think our oceans are so huge that they could never become badly polluted. Unfortunately, this is not the case. At the end of a river's journey, it will dump all its pollution into the sea. This pollution can kill or drive away sea creatures that live near river mouths and coasts. The sea can also be polluted by container ships that carry garbage and waste materials from factories. The ships dump their poisonous cargo into the ocean.

Oil spillage

Some of the worst ocean pollution comes from modern supertankers, which are over 1,500 feet (457 meters) long. They carry more than 500,000 short tons (450,000 metric tons) of oil. If a supertanker runs aground or breaks up in rough seas, it quickly creates a major disaster as the oil spills over the surface of the sea.

Coastal oil spills are especially harmful, killing fish, sea birds, and other sea animals. Oil clogs their scales and feathers so that they cannot move. Birds often swallow the poisonous oil when they try to clean it from their feathers.

This bird can't fly because its feathers are covered in oil. Although rescuers try to clean off the oil, many birds die in oil spills.

Garbage thrown overboard from ships litters the shoreline.

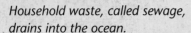

Household waste, called sewage, drains into the ocean.

Poisoning the food chain

Ocean fish take in chemicals from polluted sea water and poisoned plants. If the fish survive, they may be eaten by other animals. In turn, these animals will be poisoned. The poison is carried through the food chain.

Tiny living creatures called bacteria in sewage and other waste products multiply quickly in the ocean. The bacteria use up valuable oxygen in the water. Fish and other sea animals need oxygen to breathe. They will soon die from lack of oxygen if the ocean becomes too polluted.

Dangerous wastes from industry are dumped at sea in containers. The containers may decay one day and release their poisons into the water.

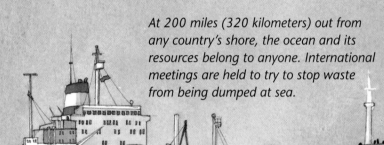

At 200 miles (320 kilometers) out from any country's shore, the ocean and its resources belong to anyone. International meetings are held to try to stop waste from being dumped at sea.

Cleaning up the water

Oil spills are often broken up using detergents. Try this for yourself.

You will need:

some oil

household detergent

a screw-top jar filled with water

1. Add a few drops of oil to the jar of water. Screw on the lid and give the jar a shake. Has the oil mixed with the water?

2. Now add a few drops of detergent to the jar. Screw the lid back on and shake the jar well. What has happened to the oil?

Find out more by looking at pages **106–107**

Explosion at Chernobyl

Nuclear power stations use a radioactive material called uranium as an energy source to make electricity. Radioactive materials give out energy called **radiation**. It is a very powerful form of energy that is absorbed by everything around it. Plants, animals, and people are affected by radiation. It attacks the cells that make up our bodies. Radiation energy remains active for a long time.

Early in the morning of April 26, 1986, alarm bells began to ring at a poorly constructed power station at Chernobyl in what is now Ukraine. Soon after, there was an explosion and fire at the power station, which sent a dangerous cloud of radioactive material into the air. As a result, many living things were exposed to dangerous levels of radiation.

Radioactive clouds swept across many parts of Europe during the days following the explosion at Chernobyl.

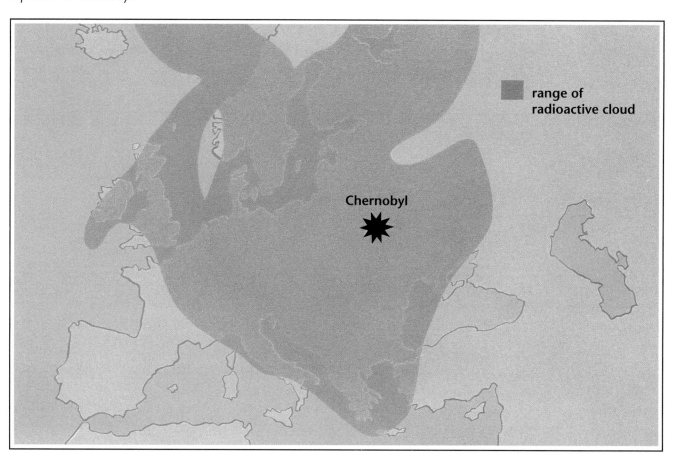

Chernobyl

range of radioactive cloud

The power station at Chernobyl was destroyed by the accident.

Scientists wearing safety clothing used Geiger counters to measure levels of radioactivity in the countryside surrounding Chernobyl.

Widespread and long-lasting damage

For a few days after the explosion, wind spread the radioactive cloud over central and northwestern Europe. Some people died as a result of the accident, and many people were seriously injured. Others are still suffering from the effects of radiation sickness. Radioactive rain fell on land where animals were grazing. After the accident, animals that had eaten radioactive grass could not be used for milk or meat. Many more people will probably die or become ill from the radioactivity, which will remain active for many years.

The world needs electricity. Nuclear power is one way of producing it. But what if there is another, even more serious accident at one of the older, Soviet-designed reactors still operating in Russia, Ukraine, and several other countries? Such accidents are possible even at power plants better constructed than the one at Chernobyl. The disposal of the radioactive waste produced by nuclear power plants is also a concern. Scientists continue to work toward developing safer and more efficient nuclear reactors.

Nuclear dump

Nuclear energy is useful. We can make electricity in nuclear power stations. In hospitals, radioactivity can help to cure some diseases. In some industries, people use radioactive substances to measure and test materials.

Radioactive material produces waste, which may be in the form of a gas, a liquid, or a solid. This waste is dangerous because it continues to emit radiation. Even small amounts of plutonium, one of the radioactive elements created in a nuclear power plant, can cause cancer. Some of it, called **high-level waste**, will be radioactive for thousands of years. **Low-level waste** is less radioactive, but scientists do not agree on how dangerous it is.

What happens to nuclear waste?

In some countries, including Japan, Russia, and the United Kingdom, the waste from nuclear power stations is sent to a nuclear reprocessing plant. The waste is then separated into different radioactive parts. Fuel and other materials are recovered. Some low-level waste is pumped into the sea, and some is buried. High-level waste is sealed in concrete and steel tanks and stored deep underground or underwater.

This is the international symbol showing that a container has radioactive material in it. If you ever see anything with this mark on it lying around, keep away from it and report it to the police.

This reprocessing plant at Sellafield in England recovers radioactive material from nuclear waste. Some low-level waste is pumped into the Irish Sea.

Waste from a nuclear power station is sent to this nuclear processing plant in La Hague, France.

Nuclear waste may be stored in solid glass.

Living with nuclear waste

It is difficult to find sites where large amounts of nuclear waste can be dumped safely. Few people want to live near a **nuclear dump.** We cannot be sure that the waste containers will not break up and leak. What would happen to them if there was an earthquake? And what if an underwater container leaked and let large amounts of radioactivity pass into the ocean?

The waste-makers

Who are the champion waste-makers of the world? This garbage pile shows the relative amount of household waste each of these countries throws away in a year. The U.S. is top of the heap—it produces more garbage than any other country in the world.

Can you imagine how much garbage we create all over the world each day? In factories, offices, hotels, and restaurants, as well as in our homes, we produce tons of garbage. Over a year, this builds up into a huge problem. Many poorer countries of the world produce the smallest amounts of garbage. In countries where there are many industries, more land is needed for garbage sites. Some of our garbage can be used again. But where can we put the rest? No one wants a garbage dump next door!

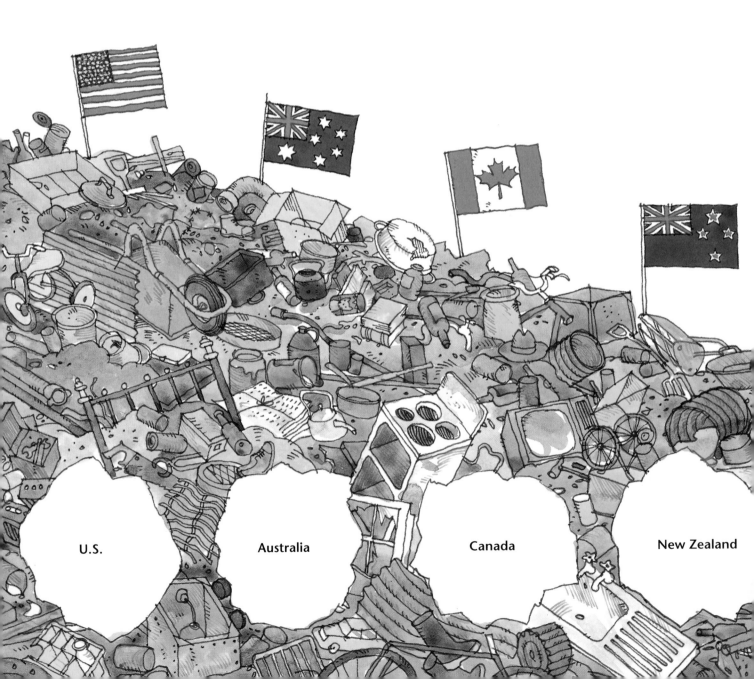

U.S.

Australia

Canada

New Zealand

Industrial waste

Waste can be burned, but this can pollute the atmosphere. It can be dumped at sea, but this pollutes the sea. There is no way of getting rid of waste that does not harm the environment in some way. Much of the waste is made in factories. When coal or other minerals are mined, waste in the form of stone and dust is brought to the surface. This is usually dumped on land in ugly mountainous heaps. The heaps can sometimes cause dangerous landslides. Other waste, produced by factories making chemicals and plastics, is poisonous. Liquid waste from factories is one of the main causes of river and lake pollution.

Waste space

Garbage must be put somewhere. Most of it is buried in old quarries or sites, and this levels out the land. When the site is full, it is covered over and often used as a building site. But that is not the end of the story. Underground, the rubbish breaks down and decays. It produces an explosive, poisonous gas called **methane**. This may escape to the surface. Rotting garbage can seep into the ground and pollute water supplies.

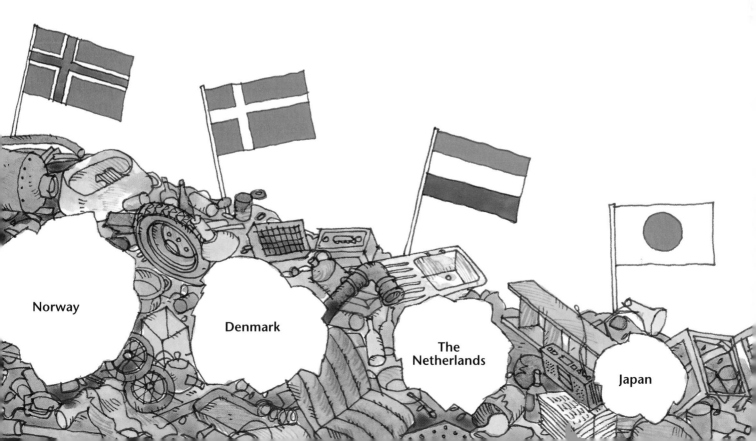

Norway

Denmark

The Netherlands

Japan

110

Find out more by looking
at pages **108–109**
112–113

Useful garbage

We make objects like paper, bottles, and cans, and then we throw them away! As time goes on, we are building up more and more garbage, which is hard to get rid of. There would be much less garbage if we saved some of the waste materials and used them again. This would also save energy because large amounts of energy are used in making new products.

New products from old

Have you ever wondered what happens to all the things we put in the garbage can? Cans, bottles, jars, cartons, newspapers, magazines, plastics, old clothes, old toys, old furniture—we throw away loads of them each year. Most of our household garbage could be used again. This is called **recycling.** Old paper, metal, and glass can be broken up and remade. Waste such as coffee grounds, potato peels, and other vegetable scraps will decay in time and can be turned into **compost.** This is a natural fertilizer for garden plants.

Here are the contents of a typical family garbage can. The newspapers can be put to one side for recycling. The jars and bottles can be taken to the recycling bin. The cans may be melted down and the metal used again. Vegetable scraps, eggshells, and coffee grounds can be put on the compost heap. That will leave only about one-fifth of the waste in the garbage can. Plastic bottles and polystyrene containers can also be added to the recycling bin. These items can be melted down and made into new products.

What about plastics?

Plastics create one of our worst waste problems. They are more difficult to recycle, because there are so many different types of plastic. Most plastics are **nonbiodegradable**, which means that they take a very long time before they begin to decay. Often, we use plastics when we don't need to. We buy food in a plastic container and then throw the container away as soon as we are home.

Recycling is one important way to reduce the amount of plastics waste. Some plastics products can be melted down and re-formed into new products. Others can be ground up into powder or shredded. The powder is used as fillers in some products. The shreds can be used to pad the inside of quilted jackets and sleeping bags.

Some communities burn plastics. They use the energy this creates for electricity and heating. But this takes special equipment.

Some plastics are now made to be **biodegradable**. Once they have been thrown away, special ingredients in the plastic cause these products to decay over time. Plastics can also be **photodegradable**. These plastics break down when they are placed in sunlight for a long period of time.

Today, many communities in the United States and Canada have curbside recycling programs along with weekly trash pickup. Recyclables are placed in specially marked containers.

How is waste recycled?

When you recycle materials, you are helping conservation in three ways. You are helping to lessen the damage to the environment that is caused by cutting down trees or mining raw materials. You are helping to save energy. You are also helping to cut down the problems of waste disposal.

Paper

Most paper is made from wood pulp, which comes from trees. Many trees have to be cut down to provide us with newspapers. That is bad enough, but large amounts of energy are used to turn the wood pulp into paper and to bleach it to make the paper white. This process releases chemicals into our rivers and so causes water pollution.

Recycled paper must first have the ink taken out. It is then turned into pulp and pressed back into sheets of paper. Recycled paper is as good as new paper, although it is a little rougher and not as white. Only about one-quarter of the world's paper is recycled. At least another quarter could be saved. Paper can also be recycled and used to make papier-mâché.

Glass

Huge amounts of energy are used in making glass, because very high temperatures are needed to melt down all the ingredients. If bottles and jars are thrown away when they are empty, all that energy is lost. But new bottles and jars can be made out of a mixture of new glass and old, broken glass, which is called cullet. This saves up to one-quarter of the energy needed to make new glass.

Metals

Metal cans are made of aluminum, or steel coated with tin, or a mixture of these metals. Aluminum cans are the most valuable to recycle. In the United States, over half of all aluminum cans are recycled. Aluminum is made from an ore called **bauxite**, which has to be electrically heated to a high temperature. Recycling saves 95 percent of the energy needed to make new aluminum cans.

Recycling paper

Paper is quite easy to recycle. Try to do it for yourself.

You will need:

some used construction paper or newspaper

a cloth

a fork

some water

a saucepan

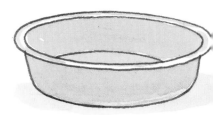

a large bowl

a flat-bottomed sieve

1. Tear the paper into small pieces and put them into a saucepan. Fill the saucepan halfway with water. Let the paper soak overnight.

2. If the paper has soaked up all the water, add some more. Mash the soggy paper with a fork until it has broken up into a mushy pulp.

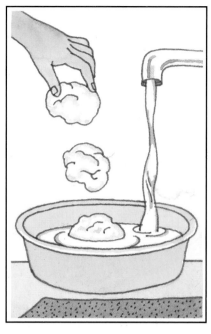

3. Fill the bowl halfway with water and add two handfuls of paper pulp. Stir the mixture well. Put a damp cloth beside the bowl.

4. Dip your sieve upside down under the water and bring it up. Hold it above the bowl until most of the water has drained away.

5. Turn the sieve right side up on the damp cloth and rock the sieve gently back and forth until the paper pulp peels away.

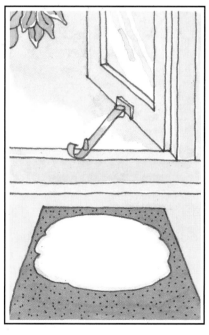

6. Spread the pulp as thinly and evenly as possible over the cloth. Leave the pulp in an airy place to dry.

The Green family

Everyone can help with conservation. The Green family, who live in this house, have thought carefully about saving energy. This means that they also save money—and eat healthier food, too. Not every family can take all these steps, but all of us can do something to help.

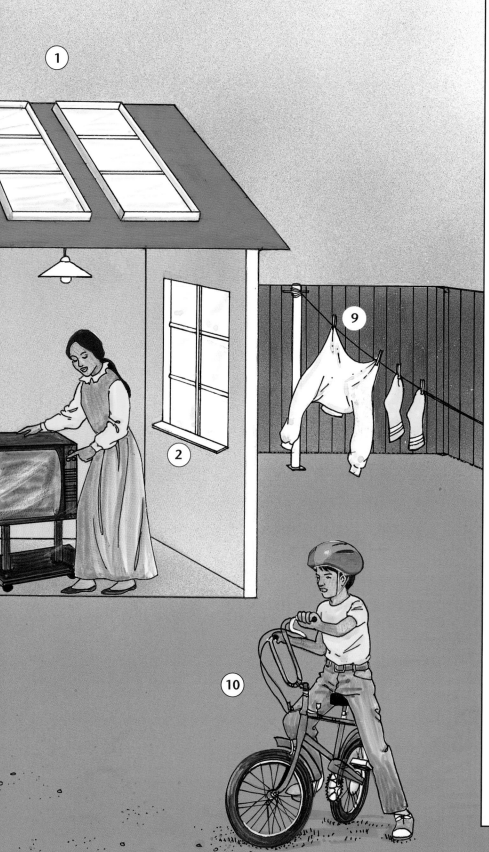

1. Solar panels on the roof collect heat from the sun. These provide the house with hot water.

2. Windows are double-glazed to keep the heat in when it is cold, and to keep the house cool in hot weather.

3. Insulation around the hot-water tank prevents heat from escaping.

4. Lights are switched off in rooms not being used.

5. Dripping faucets waste water. All the faucets are turned off properly.

6. Homemade jams and pickles are cheaper and healthier than store-bought ones. The jars can be used again and again.

7. Separate cans are used for organic waste, paper, glass, aluminum, and other garbage.

8. Organic waste is used for compost.

9. Laundry is dried in the open air instead of in an electric dryer. This saves energy.

10. Bicycles are used instead of the car for short journeys, to save energy and reduce air pollution.

11. The family car is driven only when necessary, to conserve fuel. It is kept well-tuned, and the tires are always inflated properly.

The green land

In an ideal world people would do all they could to conserve Earth's resources.

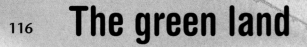

Used glass, metals, and paper are collected so that they can be recycled.

River and ocean water are not polluted and are safe for swimming and other water sports.

Farm animals are kept outside instead of in factory farms. They are fed partly on feed made from organic waste.

Farmers rotate their crops. This helps to keep the soil fertile, and fewer chemical fertilizers are needed.

Cycle tracks on roads make it safer for cyclists.

There are recycling bins for used glass and old cans.

All cars use lead-free gasoline and their exhaust systems are designed to "clean" the fumes. Cars are rustproofed, too, so that they last longer.

Woodland is harvested and replanted carefully to preserve wildlife habitats.

Wind generators provide electricity for farms and houses in remote places.

Factory chimneys have filters to prevent pollution from reaching the atmosphere.

Small parks provide wildlife habitats in towns.

A rapid-transport light railroad takes people to and from work, school, and shopping. People leave their cars at home to reduce pollution from traffic.

Acid rain: Substance that forms when moisture in the air combines with certain chemicals released by automobiles, factories, and power plants that burn coal or oil. This substance falls to the ground with rain or snow.

Alley cropping: Farming method by which trees and crops are mixed on the same piece of land.

Antibody: Substance in a human being's or animal's body that fights disease.

Artery: Blood vessel that carries oxygen-rich blood away from the heart and to the rest of the body.

Axon: Longer branch of the *nerve cell* that carries messages out of the nerve cell and connects with other nerve cells in the body. Some axons pass their messages on to different parts of the body.

Bacteria: Small living thing that can live inside the body and cause disease.

Biodegradable: Able to decay.

Blood vessel: Tube through which blood travels in the body.

Cancer: Disease caused by cells that grow and divide without control.

Capillary: Tiny tubelike vessel in the body through which blood flows.

Cartilage: Smooth, rubbery substance that covers the ends of bones. It works like a cushion so that bones don't grind together.

Cell: Tiny unit of living matter that makes up all animals and plants.

Chlorofluorocarbon: Harmful chemical once used in aerosol cans that causes substances, such as polish or deodorant, to shoot out of the can.

Coal: Black substance that forms in the earth from decayed matter.

Compost: Natural fertilizer made from waste. It is used to help garden plants grow.

Conservation: Careful use of something, especially a natural resource, to help protect Earth and its resources.

Contour plowing: Farming method by which crops are plowed across a slope instead of up and down it. This helps prevent water from wearing away the soil.

Crop rotation: Farming method by which different crops are planted on the same piece of land at different times.

Cytoplasm: Jellylike substance that all cells are made of.

Dendrite: Shorter branch of nerve cells that takes in messages from other nerve cells.

Dermis: Second layer of skin, where the nerves and sweat glands are found.

Digestion: Process that breaks down food in the body.

Drought: Long period without rain.

Endangered species: Animal group in danger of dying out.

Energy: Force having the power to make things move or work.

Enzyme: Chemical in the body that helps break down food.

Epidermis: Top layer of skin.

Fertilizer: Substance added to soil to help crops grow well.

Fossil fuel: Energy developed from the remains of prehistoric plants and animals. Fossil fuels include coal, natural gas, and petroleum, from which we get oil.

Greenhouse effect: Behavior of Earth's atmosphere that causes heat from the sun to be trapped near Earth's surface.

Habitat: Home to many living things, both plants and animals.

Hemoglobin: Substance in red blood cells that carries oxygen from the lungs to other parts of the body.

Hormone: Chemical that helps to control such body functions as growth, development, and reproduction.

Humus: Substance made from dead plant matter.

Hydroelectric power: Energy that comes from falling water.

Immune system: Network of cells that keep the body healthy most of the time by fighting invaders such as *bacteria* and *viruses.*

Intensive agriculture: Farming method by which huge areas of land are plowed and planted with crops year after year.

Joint: Place where bones meet. Joints make it possible for the body to move.

Kidney: Organ that filters waste and salts from blood. Kidneys make urine, the body's waste liquid. There are two kidneys, one on each side of the spine.

Ligament: Strong, flexible strap that holds bones or other body parts together.

Liver: Body organ that removes some nutrients from the blood and stores them until they are needed. The liver also changes some nutrients into other substances that the body uses.

Marrow: Soft tissue in the hollow center of long bones. There are two kinds of marrow—red and yellow. Red marrow makes fresh blood cells and yellow marrow is mostly fat.

Natural resource: Something that Earth provides.

Nerve cell: Cell that uses impulses of electricity to carry messages throughout the body.

Nutrient: Any substance, such as food, that is nourishing and promotes growth and good health. Cells need nutrients to survive.

Organ: Part of the body that is made up of tissue joined together. Eyes, the heart, and the brain are examples of organs.

Ozone layer: Layer of gas that surrounds Earth. Ozone shields Earth from some of the dangerous rays of the sun.

Periosteum: Strong substance that covers bones.

Pesticide: Chemical substance used to kill pests.

Photodegradable: Able to decay with long exposure to sunlight.

Poacher: Illegal hunter of animals.

Protein: Food substance necessary for the growth and maintenance of body structures.

Protist: Soft, jellylike creature that invades the body and causes disease.

Radiation: Energy given out by *radioactive* materials. It is a very powerful form of energy that is absorbed by everything around it.

Radioactive: Having energy that is created by atoms breaking up.

Recycling: Process by which waste is used again.

Red blood cell: Cell that carries oxygen from the lungs to the body tissues.

Reflex: An automatic movement that does not involve the brain.

Solar energy: Energy from the light of the sun.

Spinal cord: Thick bundle of nerves that runs down the back inside the backbone and carries messages from the brain to the rest of the body.

Synovial fluid: Liquid that covers *cartilage,* keeping bones moving smoothly, like oil in the parts of a machine.

Tissue: Cells of the same kind and function joined together.

Tropical rain forest: Huge, dense forest where it is hot and wet. Trees and plants grow very quickly in a tropical rain forest.

Ultraviolet ray: Invisible form of light. The sun is the major source of ultraviolet rays.

Vein: Blood vessel that returns the blood to the heart.

Vibration: Tiny, rapid movement back and forth or up and down.

Virus: Tiny living thing that can live inside the body and cause disease.

White blood cell: Cell that kills germs that enter the body.

Acknowledgements

The publishers of **World Book's** *Young Scientist* acknowledge the following photographers, publishers, agencies, and corporations for photographs used in this volume.

Cover	© PhotoDisc, Inc.
2/7	© PhotoDisc, Inc.
8/9	© Antman, The Image Works
10/11	© Secchi Lecaque, Science Photo Library
18/19	© Eric Grave, Science Photo Library
28/29	© Melanie Friend, Hutchison Library
38/39	© Spectrum Colour Library
42/43	© Norman Myers, Bruce Coleman Collection
44/45	© Ellen Senisi, The Image Works
46/47	© Petit Format/Nestlé from Science Photo Library
48/49	© Science Photo Library
50/51	© Biophoto Associates from Science Photo Library
52/53	© David R. Frazier
54/55	© Martin Dohrn, Science Photo Library
58/59	© St. Bartholomew's Hospital from Science Photo Library; © Bruce Coleman Collection
60/61	© Sunak, ZEFA Picture Library; © D. and J. McClurg, Bruce Coleman Collection
64/65	© ZEFA Picture Library; © Bruce Coleman Collection
66/67	© Science Photo Library; © Bruce Coleman Collection
68/69	© ZEFA Picture Library
72/73	© Rod Williams, Bruce Coleman Collection; © L. C. Marigo, Bruce Coleman Collection
76/77	© M. J. Thomas, Frank Lane Picture Agency
78/79	© L. C. Marigo, Bruce Coleman Collection
80/81	© Loren McIntyre, Susan Griggs Agency; © Elizabeth Kemf
88/89	© Mark Boulton, Bruce Coleman Collection; © B. Peterson, ZEFA Picture Library
90/91	© David Nunuk/SPL from Photo Researchers
94/95	© Eric Crichton, Bruce Coleman Collection
100/101	© Everts, ZEFA Picture Library
104/105	© Igor Kostin, Corbis Sygma; © Frank Spooner Picture Agency
106/107	© ZEFA Picture Library; © Y. Arthus-Bertrand, Peter Arnold, Inc.; West Valley Nuclear Services Co.
110/111	© Ericka Stone, Photo Researchers

Illustrated by

Martin Aitchinson
Nigel Alexander
Hemesh Alles
Martyn Andrews
Sue Barclay
Richard Berridge
John Booth
Lou Bory
Maggie Brand
Stephen Brayfield
Bristol Illustrators
Colin Brown
Estelle Carol
David Cook
Marie DeJohn
Richard Deverell
Farley, White and Veal
Sheila Galbraith
Peter Geissler
Jeremy Gower
Kathie Kelleher
Stuart Lafford

John Lobban
Louise Martin
Annabel Milne
Yoshi Miyake
Donald Moss
Eileen Mueller Neill
Teresa O'Brien
Paul Perreault
Roberta Polfus
Jeremy Pyke
Trevor Ridley
Barry Rowe
Don Simpson
Gary Slater
Lawrie Taylor
Gwen Tourret
Pat Tourret
Peter Visscher
David Webb
Gerald Whitcomb
Matthew White
Lynne Willey